THE SOCIAL TEACHING
OF ST PAUL

THE SOCIAL TEACHING

OF ST PAUL

BY

W. EDWARD CHADWICK, B.D. (Camb.), B.Sc. (Vict.)

LATE FOUNDATION SCHOLAR OF JESUS COLLEGE, CAMBRIDGE ;
VICAR OF ST GILES', NORTHAMPTON.

Author of "The First Church Workers"; "The Work of the
Church in Suburban Parishes"; etc. etc.

CAMBRIDGE

AT THE UNIVERSITY PRESS

1906

CAMBRIDGE
UNIVERSITY PRESS

University Printing House, Cambridge CB2 8BS, United Kingdom

Published in the United States of America by Cambridge University Press, New York

Cambridge University Press is part of the University of Cambridge.

It furthers the University's mission by disseminating knowledge in the pursuit of
education, learning and research at the highest international levels of excellence.

www.cambridge.org
Information on this title: www.cambridge.org/9781107416017

© Cambridge University Press 1906

First published 1906
First paperback edition 2014

A catalogue record for this publication is available from the British Library

ISBN 978-1-107-41601-7 Paperback

TO MY WIFE

Wellhausen schreibt : "Durch Paulus besonders hat sich das Evangelium vom Reich in das Evangelium von Jesu Christo verwandelt, so dass es nicht mehr die Weissagung des Reichs, sondern die durch Jesus Christus geschehene Erfüllung dieser Weissagung ist."

HARNACK, *Das Wesen*, p. 111.

"We cannot doubt that God is calling us in this age, through the characteristic teachings of science and of history, to seek a new social application of the Gospel."

BISHOP WESTCOTT.

"Zeal, enthusiasm, devotion are not enough to guide us in the perplexity of Conduct ; we need above all things knowledge as the basis of action."

BISHOP WESTCOTT.

"Das Evangelium ist eine soziale Botschaft von heiligem Ernst und erschütternder Kraft ; es ist die Verkündigung der Solidarität und Brüderlichkeit....Aber diese Botschaft ist verbunden mit der Anerkennung des unendlichen Wertes der Menschenseele."

HARNACK, *Das Wesen*, p. 65.

CONTENTS.

PREFATORY NOTE.

IN the following pages I have not attempted to give either a complete account of St Paul's Social Teaching, or a final estimate of its contents. The task I have set before me is a much humbler one. All I have tried to do is, 1st, to point out certain factors in that teaching which must be carefully considered before either such an account can be given, or such an estimate can be formed; and 2nd, to show how very close is the agreement between St Paul's social principles and those principles of social welfare which modern students of Sociology, working by the inductive method, have, as they believe, discovered.

I have not considered it necessary to enter into the question of the authenticity of the letters which bear St Paul's name. To have discussed this subject at length, to have stated the arguments for and against each separate epistle, and to have quoted the various authorities for each view in each particular case, would have unduly lengthened my essay. Upon such a subject any treatment less than the fullest possible can hardly be satisfactory. For two other reasons I have decided to omit it, (1) such a discussion can be readily found elsewhere[1], (2) the absolute authenticity of each letter is not essential for my argument. Even if some of the letters be not St Paul's they all represent his *teaching*, and this may be said to be sufficient for my present purpose.

[1] A very recent and luminous statement of the present position of the question may be found in Dr Knowling's *The Testimony of St Paul to Christ*, pp. 3–16.

W. E. C.

May 1906.

INTRODUCTION.

ONLY within the last few years has any serious attempt been made to investigate the 'social' teaching of the New Testament in order to apply this teaching towards the solution of modern social problems. For this delay in the working of a field which may be expected to yield rich and useful fruit, at least three reasons may be given:—

(1) The widespread interest which we are witnessing in the many different 'problems,' which together form the one great 'Social Problem,' is itself of comparatively recent growth.

(2) The 'Gospel,' so far as it has been regarded as a 'power unto salvation' (in the widest sense of the words), has in the past been too generally regarded as containing primarily, if not exclusively, a message to, and for, the individual.

(3) Where there has been any examination of the New Testament in order to investigate the nature of the community-life of the first Christians, this examination has generally been made from some particular ecclesiastical point of view, and primarily with the object of fortifying and establishing some preconceived theory of the organisation of the Christian Community during its earliest years[1].

[1] Bigg, *The Church's Task under the Roman Empire*, pp. vii. ff.

To some extent it may for a long time have been realised that "according to the New Testament the Christian life is the true human life, and that Christians become true men in proportion as they live up to it[1]"; but only lately have we begun to discover that the New Testament is full of 'social' ideals—themselves parts of the one social Ideal: in other words, that "the right relations between members of the Christian Society are simply the normal relations which should exist between members of the human race[2]." Or, as Professor Ramsay expresses the same thought, "St John always assumes that the Church is in a sense the city....The Church is all that is real in the city; the rest of the city has failed to reach its true self, and has been arrested in its development[3]."*

Recently, however, one most important part of the Social Teaching of the New Testament has been carefully examined. I refer to the Social Teaching of our Lord Himself. With the advent of 'the Social

[1] Hort, *Christian Ecclesia*, p. 228.

[2] *Ibid.*

[3] *The Letters to the Seven Churches*, p. 41.

* The following is probably an additional reason for the neglect of the Social Teaching of the New Testament. The Study of Sociology as a science has been much neglected, especially in England. Even now in England Sociology cannot be said to have won for itself an assured position among the exact sciences. Consequently it has not been noticed that much of the Social Teaching of the New Testament (if couched in old-world, and to some extent 'unscientific,' language) consists of fundamental Sociological Laws, and these expressed as guides to human conduct. [See Additional Note on 'The Realism of St Paul,' p. 142.]

Question'—and that advent is due to a variety of causes—we have been compelled to learn how important a question it is; and how far-reaching in their consequences must inevitably be the answers which are given to it. This being so it is only natural that men are asking, "What answer, or answers does 'Christianity' give to the many problems with which we are being faced?" In order to meet this demand the Social Teaching of our Lord, both as a whole and in regard to various particular relations of social life, has been examined in a number of books devoted expressly to this purpose[1].

But if every word and action of our Lord which bears, however remotely, upon the social question were adequately examined—if the whole of His personal teaching on the subject were clearly set forth—we should not then be in possession of 'The Social Teaching of Christianity.' As Harnack has so clearly pointed out, a complete answer to the question, 'What is Christian?' must take into consideration at least the teaching of the first generation of our Lord's followers[2]. Among these, in wide experience of very different social conditions, St Paul probably stands preeminent. He was the first of the New Testament writers to propagate Christianity upon the wide field of the Graeco-Roman world[3], and he was the first called upon to apply the principles of Christianity to social conditions far more diversified and complex than those described for us in the Gospels. Thus, in any attempt

---

[1] *e.g.* Peabody, *Jesus Christ and the Social Question.*
[2] *Das Wesen*, p. 6.
[3] Wernle, *Die Anfänge*, p. 96.

to state the 'Social Teaching' of 'Christianity' that of St Paul must claim the most careful consideration. Yet, as far as I am aware, no attempt has been made to deal with this subject as a connected whole; though in multitudes of notes by commentators upon the Acts and his Epistles, and also in many passages of books upon St Paul's life and teaching, as well as upon the age in which he worked, there is a wealth of material helpful for this purpose.

The subject of St Paul's Social Teaching is a large one, and very soon after I entered upon an examination of it I found it would be necessary to impose upon myself certain definite limits. These will be clear when I state that all I have attempted is as follows:—

(i) I have tried to show that from our knowledge of St Paul's history previous to his conversion we may assume, first, that he had an intimate knowledge of the *actual* social conditions of both the Jewish and the Gentile world, as these existed in such cities as Tarsus and Jerusalem: secondly, that he must have been familiar (a) with social *ideals* which at that time inspired various sections[1] of the Jewish people; (β) with ideals which must have entered the mind of a native of a "city renowned for its educational advantages, and proud of its Greek culture and uncommon devotion to intellectual pursuits[2]," a city which also was one of the strongholds of the Stoic Philosophy; and (γ) with ideals which cannot have

[1] The forms of the Messianic hope conceived by the educated and uneducated Jews were apparently widely different.

[2] McGiffert, *History of Christianity in the Apostolic Age*, p. 113.

failed to influence a Roman citizen who, with quite
pardonable pride, was always ready to claim the
privileges to which that citizenship entitled him.

(ii) I have tried to show that in St Paul's speeches
and letters we have evidence of what may be termed a
re-reading of the Old Testament in the light of the new
knowledge and new convictions which produced his
'conversion'; and how in this light the social teaching
of the Prophets of Israel became filled with (at any
rate to him) a new significance[1].

(iii) I have tried to show how, as a result of this
're-reading' of the Old Testament, the Messianic
teaching and hopes, both of his forefathers and contemporaries, not only as these referred to a Messianic
King and a Messianic *Age*, but as they referred to a
Messianic *Society* acquired for St Paul a higher and
fuller meaning.

(iv) I have sought, by a brief study of some
passages chosen from his Epistles, to explain a few
of the leading ideas in St Paul's conception of the
Social teaching and Social possibilities of Christianity.

Between St Paul's social teaching and the highest
social aspirations and efforts of the present day there
are, I believe, two strong affinities.

(1) In both we find a common note of *intense
earnestness*. This was probably the dominant element
in St Paul's character[2]; it was also the strongest link
in that chain of personal piety which bound together
his earlier and his later life. It makes us feel that,

---

[1] G. A. Smith, *Isaiah*, ii. 287 ff.

[2] Acts xxii. 3, Gal. i. 14, Philipp. iii. 6, 2 Cor. iv. 7 ff.

however different were his attitudes towards Christ
and Christianity before and after his conversion—that
of the zealous persecuting Pharisee and of the equally
zealous Christian Missionary—both were inspired by
an intense 'zeal for God.' The earnestness in both
periods was that of the same man, but the efforts
towards which it drove him were directed towards
different, and apparently opposite, purposes. But in
both periods we have before us a man so convinced
that he has a 'mission' that he is prepared to exercise
the 'totality of his powers' towards its accomplish-
ment. Then it probably was not simply on account of
the strangeness of the theories (or doctrines) which
they preached, but because of the earnestness or zeal
with which they preached them, and strove to put
them into effect, that St Paul and his companions were
charged as enemies of the social order[1]. In the First
Epistle of St Peter[2]—which was addressed to the
Christians of those districts where St Paul's influence
may be assumed to have been most strong—its readers
are more than once warned to be specially careful of

[1] ἐκταράσσουσιν, Acts xvi. 20; οἰκουμένην ἀναστατώσαντες, Acts
xvii. 6.

[2] e.g. iii. 16, iv. 15, 16 (vide Prof. Bigg's note on ἀλλοτριοεπίσκοπος,
who compares ἀλλότρια πολυπραγμονεῖ in Epictet. iii. 22, 97): and
adds "a Christian might give great offence by ill-timed protests
against common social customs." Note also W. W. Capes, The Age
of the Antonines, p. 137 : "Much might seem dangerous in the
mysterious influence of the new religion. Its talk of equality and
brotherhood might sound like the watchword of a social revolution.
...The ties of sympathy between its scattered members were like
the network of a widespread conspiracy, whose designs might be
political."

their conduct lest this charge of being social revolutionaries be brought against them.

As the result of a similar earnestness, and of a zeal which, like that of the early Christians, is not always tempered by discretion, the same charge—of being 'revolutionaries'—is to-day brought against numbers of men who by the study of the social question are being stirred to the very depths of their being. If we consider the changes wrought both in the ideas and constitution of society through Christian influences, from the first century to the present time, these changes amount to nothing less than a revolution. As to how much farther this revolution might with advantage still proceed opinions differ. Of the *earnestness* with which many social reformers to-day are pressing for drastic changes there can be no doubt. "The literature of the present age is saturated with the desire for social revolution[1]." "The party of revolution, with its millions of voters in many European countries, officially announces that all other issues are to be subordinated to the social question[1]." "Beneath all the tranquillizing arrangements of philanthropy or industry, which are being applied to social disorder, there is a vast and rising tide of discontent stirring to its very bottom the stream of social life[1,2]." Much of the social effort of to-day, especially on the Continent, is, of course, at least on the surface, frankly anti-Christian, though underlying it there is probably

[1] Peabody, *Jesus Christ and the Social Question*, p. 6.

[2] I give these quotations simply to show how intensely *earnest* are the men who have provoked, and who are still stirring up, this flood of discontent.

more unconscious[1] Christianity than its promoters would admit. And there is not less earnestness among those social workers who are working on definite Christian lines, and who are inspired by definite Christian principles. The numerous 'Settlements' in the poorest parts of London and our other large towns, as well as the immense number of efforts and movements directed against particular social evils, bear witness to the same fact.

(2) The second great mark of similarity between St Paul's social teaching and the social movement of the present day is the strong *ethical* basis of both.

Equally with his earnestness, St Paul's intense 'zeal for righteousness' was common to the two great periods of his life. However different may have been his conceptions of the contents and aim of righteousness before and after his conversion, we may safely assert that the highest ethical ideal, in purpose and in conduct, was throughout his life the motive power of all his actions[2,3].

---

[1] Possibly in this particular the present social movement offers more than one interesting parallel to certain movements which were contemporaneous with, or which rather followed upon, the religious upheaval in Germany during the first half of the sixteenth century. (See *The Cambridge Modern History*, Vol. ii. pp. 184 ff.)

[2] Acts xxii. 3, Philipp. iii. 6.

[3] "In every page of Paul's writings that restless, self-conceited, morbid, unhealthy society" (*i.e.* of the Graeco-Asiatic cities) "stands out in strong relief before the reader. He knew it so well because he was born and brought up in its midst. He conceived that his mission was to regenerate it, and the plan which he saw to be the only possible one was to save the Jew from sinking down to the pagan level, by elevating the pagan to the true (N.B. *true*, cf.

When, as a member of the Cilician Synagogue he was among those who disputed with Stephen, the very charges which he assisted in bringing against Stephen (and it is incredible that he knew these to be false) were charges of being an enemy to 'righteousness[1].' To speak lightly against Moses was, in St Paul's eyes, evidently tantamount to speaking lightly against God —the author of all righteousness; so 'to speak words against this holy place and the law' was to speak against the one place on earth whence a fountain of righteousness issued, and against the one standard by which righteousness could be safely estimated. To 'change the customs delivered by Moses' was to abolish the whole series of actions in personal and social life which to a Pharisee were the ultimate test of righteousness in conduct. Saul the Pharisee may have had an entirely false conception of 'righteousness,' but it is impossible, in the face of his own description of his 'former life,' to compare his motives in attacking Christ and His followers with those which actuated Annas and Caiaphas and the Sadducean hierarchy.

The same sense of a 'call' on behalf of righteousness inspires the thoughtful and earnest social worker at the present time. In two ways this may be seen.

Rom. ii. 17, 18, 28, 29) Jewish level." (Ramsay, *Seven Churches*, p. 135.)

"The salutary idea which was needed to keep the Empire sound and the cities healthy was what Paul preached; and that was the raising of the Gentiles to equality with the Jews in religion and morality." *Ibid.* p. 141.

[1] Acts vi. 11 ff.

(1) At the basis of all social movements there lies the idea of a wrong—an injustice[1], an 'unrighteousness'—to be righted. There is a growing consciousness of contradiction between much which exists in the actual economic conditions of the present, and the spiritual ideals which inspire noble minds. This consciousness often utters itself in a passionate cry of indignation. (2) It is being more and more clearly realised by social leaders and workers that the problem which must be solved is rather an *ethical*[2], than a purely economic one. They see that it is to an improvement in character and aim of life, in other words, to an increase of righteousness, that effort must be directed, rather than, primarily, to improve economic resources or to give greater spending power.

The present 'social' situation seems to offer yet another interesting parallel to that in the midst of which St Paul laboured. The 'social movement' on the Continent, *e.g.* in Germany, France, Italy, contains it must be admitted certain strong ethical elements, yet it is generally regarded as distinctly anti-Christian[3]. [But would not 'anti-clerical,' or 'anti-ecclesiastical'[4] be a truer definition of its spirit?] The more thoughtful observer may, however, see in it, not a necessarily

---

[1] "The power and pathos of the modern social movement reside in the passionate demand, now heard on every hand, for Justice...the chance for a human way of life." [Peabody, p. 10.]

[2] "The Social Question of the present time is an ethical question." [Peabody, p. 9.]

[3] Peabody, pp. 15, 16.

[4] See *The Brass-workers of Berlin and Birmingham*, p. 19.

anti-religious movement, but an attempt to substitute another religion for Christianity, as this is generally understood and expressed. But may not this new (social) religion contain more Christianity than those who propagate it suspect? May it not make prominent certain elements in Christianity which have for a long time been unheeded or neglected?

Now in the following chapters, among other tasks which I have set myself I shall try to show how St Paul, in his propagation of Christianity (which he did with the Old Testament in his hand[1]), made prominent, indeed very frequently he actually based his appeal upon, certain elements in the Old Testament which, if not entirely neglected by his contemporaries and immediate predecessors in Judaism, were yet treated by them as of quite secondary importance. I refer to the teaching of the prophets and, in a less degree, to that of the psalmists. And even when these were read and explained, their true meaning, and especially their *social* application, was ignored. The Jew regarded St Paul as an enemy to his religion. What St Paul was actually guilty of was that he turned from the ceremonial and external demands of 'the Law'; and, in the light, and under the inspiration, of Christianity, he uttered the great message of ethical and social *righteousness* which the prophets of Israel had preached. In the social movement in England there is far less direct antagonism than upon the

---

[1] " The Old Testament invests social, economic, political problems with a sacred dignity. The voices of lawgiver and prophet guide us to their eternal lessons." [Westcott, *Christian Aspects of Life*, p. 238.]

Continent to the popular expression of Christianity —that which is given in the life of 'the Churches.' In the social movement in this country we have rather a development of certain factors (or, perhaps, rather possibilities) of the Christianity of the New Testament. If, as I believe, St Paul was called to discern the wonderful possibilities in the direction of social application of the teaching of our Lord (that is of the fundamental principles of Christianity), we have again a likeness between St Paul's position and that of the Christian social teacher of the present day[1].

It is in the hope of making more clear what St Paul's Social Teaching actually was, and of showing how applicable it is to solve the problems, and to supply the needs, of the present, that the following examination has been undertaken.

---

[1] " Touched by a new sense of social obligation, we shall recognize that it is for us to bring the latest teachings of our Faith to bear with sobering, chastening, sustaining force on the thoughts and aspirations of our fellow men." [Bp. Westcott, *Christian Aspects of Life*, p. 226.]

CHAPTER I.

THE PREPARATION OF ST PAUL FOR HIS WORK.

A. GENERALLY.

[1]THE entrance of new ideas into any man's mind is conditioned by, or dependent upon, his previous knowledge and experience, that is, upon the ideas *already* within his consciousness. A man may have a remarkable gift for idealisation; his powers of imagination may be of a high order, his 'faith' may be extremely strong, his ability to 'develope' ideas may be exceptionally great, but the *materials* upon which, and through which, these various powers and faculties act can only be such as already lie within his consciousness. These materials are his *ideas*, which are the fruit of his knowledge, gained either through study

[1] The reason for this, and the following paragraph, may be found in Pfleiderer's remark : " In der That hat man auch von jeher über die psychologische Vermittlung oder Vorbereitung der Bekehrung Pauli Hypothesen aufgestellt; nur freilich waren sie solange von wenig Werth, als es an jedem Kanon zur Beurtheilung ihrer Wahrscheinlichkeit fehlte. Einen solchen haben wir nun aber damit gewonnen, dass wir in den psychologischen Prämissen der Bekehrung Pauli zugleich die Wurzeln seines eigenthümlichen Evangeliums suchen." (*Paulinismus*, Zweite Auflage, p. 4.)

or personal experience. His study and his personal
experience together form his *education*, in the most
comprehensive sense of the word, and in education
the religious, social, political, and intellectual 'atmo-
spheres' (I include in these the influence of 'tradition'),
in which a man is brought up, form the most important
factors.

A very great change may take place in the 'spirit'
of a man's life; and the direction in which his energies
are expended may be entirely altered: this change, as
far as others can judge, may be a very sudden one—as
sudden as the bursting into activity of a new volcano—
and the outward tenour of the life may be almost
entirely altered: but this revolution in opinion and
conduct must be regarded as the explosion of forces
which, through the more or less gradual assimilation
of new ideas, have long been accumulating[1]. The final
change—the visible and practical breach with the man's
past conduct—may be the result of some definite overmastering condition, which may be actually 'timed'
to the reading of a particular book, the meeting and
argument with a stranger, or the hearing of a sermon;
but the possibility of this change, or conviction, and
the results which issue from it, are 'conditioned' by
the contents of the subject's consciousness at the time
when the new knowledge or the new ideas enter it.
A study of Psychology also shows us that while new
ideas can only enter a mind through the existence in
that mind of more or less closely or remotely related
ideas, yet, when the new ideas do enter and take

[1] Acts xxii. 13.

possession, they may so conquer and transform the old ideas that these are either almost unrecognizable as the same, or they are driven so far and so permanently into the 'margin' of the field of consciousness that they cease to be of practical importance in estimating the new condition of the contents of consciousness. It is by remembering these psychological laws or facts that we account for the different effects upon different individuals of the same new spiritual or intellectual forces. These same laws account for the different conceptions and expressions and applications of Christianity, that is, of its fundamental principles (as enunciated by our Lord), which we find in the New Testament writers[1]. As a parallel case we might cite the different expositions of Christianity, or the different conceptions of the Christian Church formed by the various Reformers[2], upon whom the same flood of new knowledge streamed, in the early part of the sixteenth century.

We may divide St Paul's life into three periods[3]:—

(1) From his birth to the time when he first came under the influence of Christianity, that is, when Christianity first became known to him and he placed himself in antagonism to it.

---

[1] *e.g.* St James, St John, and St Paul.

[2] *e.g.* Luther, Erasmus, John Calvin, etc.

[3] From another point of view, Thackeray (*St Paul and Contemp. Jewish Thought*) divides St Paul's life into three periods: (i) A state of unconsciousness to the claims of the Law, Rom. vii. 9. (ii) A Life under the Constraint of Law. (iii) A Life of Freedom from Law, when he can speak of himself as "under law to Christ" (1 Cor. ix. 21).

(2) The period during which he was contending in his own mind or consciousness *against* the truth of the doctrines which he understood the Christian teachers (*e. g.* St Stephen) to assert. During this period he was persecuting the Christians[1].

(3) The period during which he was a convinced Christian, and when he worked as a Christian Teacher and Missionary.

At the close of the first period the ideas in St Paul's consciousness would be due to three chief sources, which may be termed, (1) the *Jewish*, (2) the *Hellenic*, and (3) the *Roman*, though not one of these sources was *pure*—untouched by influences from the other two, and even from more remote influences—when St Paul drew from them[2].

(1) The Jewish influences would come through three main channels:—(a) that of his home: he was a child of Pharisees and brought up in the tenets of that 'straitest' sect; (β) through instruction received at the feet of Gamaliel, and from other rabbinical teachers; (γ) through the 'atmosphere' in which as a young man (whether in Palestine or among the Jews of the Diaspora) he was being prepared, by association with others likeminded with himself, to become zealous for the traditions of his fathers, to become, in short, an earnest Jewish partisan. Through these various channels the chief ideas which would obtain admittance

---

[1] Upon how a man's 'environment' becomes actually part of himself see an illuminating essay, "The Faith of the Social Reformer," by Prof. Henry Jones in the *Hibbert Journal*, Jan. 1906.

[2] On St Paul's mental and doctrinal position during this period see Gore, *Romans*, Vol. i. pp. 253 ff.

into St Paul's consciousness (and so would be factors in forming his opinions and his conduct) would be due to—

(i) A knowledge of the contents of the Old Testament Scriptures, especially of the Law, but also of the messages of the great teachers of Israel, *e.g.* the Prophets, and also of the different religious, political, and social ideas of the people in the various epochs of their history.

(ii) A knowledge of the religious, political, and social condition of his countrymen, of their experiences, also of their thoughts, ideals, and aspirations, in the present and immediate past.

[Note that this second source of knowledge would probably be far more influential[1] than the first; because the vast majority of men feel far more strongly the influences of contemporary thought and ideas—the influences of the atmosphere in which they live—than they do those of the distant past, and even these influences from the past come to them charged to some extent with the atmosphere of the present. It is only the great reformers who have had the strength to break comparatively free from the influences of the present and to go back to the ideals of a purer past. This has been the power which has enabled all those 'returnings' towards the genuine or original spirit of Christianity which have taken place in the various

---

[1] Thackeray places "the influences upon St Paul" thus "in order of importance": (1) Palestinian Apocryphal Literature; (2) Rabbinic Literature; (3) Alexandrian Literature, etc. "In der Hauptsache bleibt aber die Bildung des Paulus die Bildung des Rabbinen." (Prof. Wrede, *Paulus*, p. 7.)

epochs of reform.   I must not anticipate, but I hope to
show that in his social teaching St Paul to a great
extent broke through the contemporary influences of
Rabbinic ideas and aspirations, and went back to the
great prophets of Israel, *e.g.* to the author of the
'Servant' passages in the Book of Isaiah[1].]

(2) The extent, and the relative strength of *Hellenic*
influences[2] upon St Paul's character and opinions are
much debated at the present time.   That these influences would be great we might assume from his birth
and residence at Tarsus, and this assumption is fully
justified by the contents of his Epistles.   St Paul has
been termed 'a citizen of the world[3],' and certainly
adaptability seems to have been one of the most striking features of his character; and adaptability was
certainly a Hellenic trait.   But that he borrowed his
teaching or his ideas (*e.g.* upon the *organic*[4] nature of
society) *directly* from Greek Literature would be diffi-

---

[1] G. A. Smith, *Isaiah*, Vol. ii. pp. 287–288.

A. B. Davidson on Prophecy, p. 188.   "In a very true sense
Christianity was a return to Prophetism."   Also see especially
W. Bousset, *Die Religion des Judentums*, pp. 396–397, "Wenn wir
die Gebiete...."   Again, "Im ganzen herrscht hier ein überaus weiter
Abstand zwischen der Ethik des Prophetentums und Spätjudentums."

[2] Hausrath (*Der Apostel Paulus*), and Bruce (*St Paul's Conception
of Christianity*) may be cited as among those inclined to minimise
these; whereas E. L. Hicks (in *Studia Biblica*, Vol. iv. pp. 2 ff.) and
Ramsay (*passim*) may be cited on the opposite side.   See also *Die
Christliche Freiheit, nach der Verkündigung des Apostels Paulus.*
(Johannes Weiss, p. 7.)

[3] 1 Cor. ix. 20.

[4] Sanday and Headlam's note on Rom. xii. 4 seems to be mis-
leading :—" The comparison of a social organism to a body was very
common among ancient writers."   I cannot find σῶμα used of a *social*

cult to prove. More than one attempt has been made
to show St Paul's indebtedness to the great Greek
teachers and philosophers, but we cannot trace any
direct borrowing from these. The truth is that St Paul
lived in a world saturated by Greek ideas; and St Paul
was not one to remain unaffected by his atmosphere or
environment. The influence of Hellenism upon both
Judaism and Christianity was one of the most powerful
factors in the divinely ordered preparation for the
possibility of a universal religion, and in that preparation no one had a greater share[1] than St Paul. The
process had begun long before him; but he did more
than utilize, he enormously increased the possibilities
which he found to his hand.

· The dream of Alexander the Great[2]—of a universal
Greek dominion—had already been to some extent
realised; and that dream meant a breaking down of
the barriers of race and nationality; it meant the
universal spread of the Greek language and of Greek
culture; it meant a fusion, and to some extent a
toleration of all religions. St Paul entered into the
fruits of Alexander's ideas. And, as Dr Lock[3] (quoting
Plutarch) points out, Alexander owed many of his

organism previous to St Paul's time, though *corpus* is so used by Livy.
The idea may, in St Paul's time, have been 'in the air.'   " The
comparison of men in society to the members of a body was of
course not new. With the Stoics in particular it was much in vogue."
(Hort, *Christian Ecclesia*, p. 147.)

    [1] Either as a recipient or a propagator.
    [2] Harnack's parallel and contrast, "Das Werk Alexanders des
Grossen ist zerfallen, das Werk des Paulus ist geblieben." *Das
Wesen*, p. 112.
    [3] *St Paul, the Master Builder*, pp. 27 ff.

ideas to Zeno, the reputed founder of the Stoics; and
the great influence of Stoicism upon St Paul, whatever
were the *media* of that influence, can hardly be questioned. The more we study Stoicism and the influence
it exercised, the more clearly shall we see the great
work which Stoicism did as an influence preparatory,
in more ways than one, for the Gospel[1]. Would it be
too much to assert that, among the heathen, Stoicism
fulfilled to some extent the same purpose which 'the
Law' did among the Jews[2]?

Examples of St Paul's debt to Hellenism are plen-
tifully scattered throughout his Epistles. Julicher
(*Encycl. Bib.*) instances, "The denomination of the
good as τὸ καλόν (Rom. vii. 18, 21; 2 Cor. xiii. 7; Gal.
iv. 18, etc.); the emphasis laid on virtue (ἀρετή, Phil.
iv. 8); the classification of man as pneumatic, psychic,
sarcic; the glorification of αὐτάρκεια, Phil. iv. 11, etc.
etc." Hicks (*Stud. Bib.*) notes how "Greek taught
St Paul logic, and the possibilities of abstract thinking"; how from it he borrows the examples from the
athletic games; how in a purely Greek manner he
'works up' illustrations from the Old Testament[3] in
1 Thess. v. 8, and Ephes. vi. 13.

(3) *The influence of Rome* upon St Paul must
always have been great, and no doubt it grew greater

---

[1] Johannes Weiss, *Die Christliche Freiheit*, p. 8.

[2] There are some valuable remarks on Stoicism in connection
with Christianity in Dr Bigg's *The Church's Task under the Roman
Empire*, p. xii. (Dr Bigg, I think, underrates the 'power' of
Stoicism.) There is also much valuable information on Stoicism in
Dill's *Roman Society from Nero to Marcus Aurelius, e.g.*, pp. 307 ff.

[3] Isaiah lix. 17, cf. xi. 5.

with increasing knowledge and advancing years. As he travelled from province to province he constantly saw more of that wonderful network of *organization* which touched every sphere and relation of life in so many different lands and peoples. Through his residence in Rome itself St Paul was able to become closely acquainted with the head and centre from which all these various influences issued[1], and towards which in return the resources of the provinces flowed. Lessons, allusions, analogies, and similes, directly or indirectly drawn from, or suggested by[2], the imperial system grow more frequent in his later letters; they are naturally most abundant in "the epistles of the captivity." St Paul was born in an *urbs libera et communis*, a city which was the seat of a Roman governor and where a Roman *conventus*[3] was held. He was not only a Roman citizen, but the son of a citizen. And the ease and rapidity with which he seems to have assimilated Roman influences in after years shows how well, by long familiarity with ideas connected with the Empire, his mind had been prepared for this.

For centuries the social and political system of the Church owed much to ideas connected with the Empire; but, as far as we know, St Paul was the first to see, not only the possibility of the application of these ideas, but how they might be raised and sanctified to a higher purpose. Unity in headship and in purpose[4],

[1] Eph. iv. 16, Col. ii. 19.

[2] *e.g.* Philipp. i. 13, 27, ii. 25 ; Col. ii. 15.

[3] On St Paul's knowledge of Roman Law see Hort, *Rom. and Ephes.* p. 24.

[4] Eph. iv. 4, 11, 16.

amid diversity of function; centralisation of authority
with the widest possibility of diffusion of power through
living channels[1]; absolute obedience to the head (with
protection from it) while work is being done in an
endless variety of spheres and methods; a world-wide
dominion embracing all sorts and conditions of men; a
power that rose superior to all distinctions of race, or
nation, or culture, or civilisation[2]—all these ideas, so
frequently met with in St Paul's teaching, he owed
directly or indirectly to the inspiration of Rome, while
he travelled its provinces, dwelt in its capital, enjoyed
its protection, and as a prisoner felt the strength of its
power.

It is unnecessary to dwell upon the similarity of
thought between (1) the Universalism which issued
from the individualistic Philosophies (*e.g.* Stoicism)[3],
and (2) the citizenship of the world—the practically
cosmopolitan position, as far as civilisation was concerned,—of one possessing the citizenship of Rome.
No one can study St Paul's letters without noticing his
power of holding certain great ideas side by side:—
(1) that of the possibilities of a world-wide society
which should know no limits due to race or language
or culture, (2) the immense importance of *local* purposive, or cultural, or disciplinary societies within, and

---

[1] 1 Cor. xii. 5, 6, 12.   [2] Col. iii. 11.

[3] Stoicism, practically speaking, only "came to its own" when
it became a Roman philosophy. See Grant's *Aristotle* (Vol. i.
pp. 305 ff.).

Bp. Westcott (*Christian Aspects of Life*, p. 103) writes : "The
characteristic worship of the Ephesian Artemis added the conception
of a universal religion to that of a universal state."

as forming part of the one universal society, and (3) the
great value he placed upon the *individual* life, and the
responsibility for the discharge of the duties of the individual; and how he held that the individual member
of the local society, to which as such he owed entire
duty and allegiance, was just as surely a member of
the world-wide society. For all these ideas, whatever
may have been the particular channels through which
they came to him, St Paul was, in all probability, indebted to what we mean when we speak of the influence
of Rome[1].

STOICISM. (*Additional Note.*)

I have already briefly pointed out what may be
regarded as the chief influences of 'Hellenism' upon
St Paul. I do not intend to enlarge upon these
generally, but there is one influence which I believe
is usually considered as Hellenic, and which, because it
probably had a very considerable effect upon St Paul's
social conceptions and social teaching, it will be well to

[1] There are many points of great interest brought out in Lightfoot's
Essay on 'St Paul and Seneca,' *Philippians*, pp. 270 ff. *e.g.* The
rise of the individualistic and ethical philosophies due to the con-
quests of Alexander, and hence their unnational, and therefore
universal character; the Eastern affinities of Stoicism (see Additional Note, pp. 273, 276), how "in its Latin home Stoicism became
a motive power in the world, and exhibited those practical results
to which its renown is chiefly due," etc., etc.

See also Additional Note above, ' Stoicism.'

examine at greater length—I mean the influence of Stoicism[1].

Are we justified in regarding Stoicism as simply one of the many factors of Hellenism? And did St Paul receive its influence purely through Hellenic channels—*i.e.* through the philosophical and intellectual atmosphere of Tarsus? A negative answer must probably be given to both these questions; for it is by no means certain that Stoicism had not an oriental origin; and certainly its principles show many affinities with certain phases of Semitic thought. Witness to these affinities is not wanting in the later books of the Old Testament.

Were these books influenced by Stoicism through Hellenic channels? Or did these books influence Stoicism? Or were both these books and Stoicism affected by a common influence proceeding from a source anterior to both? To these questions it seems to be difficult to give a satisfactory answer. On the other hand, as far as St Paul is concerned, we may safely assert that (1) since Tarsus was a home and stronghold of Stoic philosophy, and (2) since the ideas

---

[1] On Stoicism, and on its relation to Christianity, much valuable information may be found in Lightfoot's Essay on St Paul and Seneca (*Philippians*, pp. 270 ff.); in Mayor, *Epistle of St James*; in E. Caird, *The Evolution of Theology in the Greek Philosophers*, and in his *Evolution of Religion*; in Dill's *Roman Society from Nero to Marc. Aurel.*; in Bigg's *The Church's Task under the Roman Empire*; in the introduction to Long's, and Rendall's *Marcus Aurelius*; in Grant's *Aristotle*, Vol. i. pp. 304 ff.; and in the articles 'Stoics' in *Hastings' Bib. Dict.*, and the *Encycl. Biblica*: see also *Die Christliche Freiheit*, by Johannes Weiss.

of Gamaliel and other Pharisaic teachers showed a
strong likeness to many of the ideas of Stoicism, Stoic
influences may well have affected him through both
Greek and Jewish channels.

In considering the affinities between Stoicism and
St Paul's teaching it will again be very necessary to
limit our field of investigation. We must not try to
show in what ways Stoicism influenced St Paul's
thought generally, but how far it may have influenced
his social teaching.

In its early days Stoicism might be described as
an 'individualistic' philosophy, but in philosophy as
elsewhere extremes have a tendency to meet, and a
philosophy which originally has neither national nor
political characteristics or aims, may easily become
international. [The Christianity of the Gospels de-
veloping into the Christianity of St Paul might be
adduced as an instance of this.]

Stoicism may be regarded as one expression of a
movement far wider than itself. For the wide and
rapid diffusion of this movement the Greek language
and the Roman Empire found the means, just as they
did for the diffusion of Christianity.

It will be interesting here to consider, (1) Stoicism,
(2) the later Judaism, and (3) Christianity, as taught
by St Paul, side by side; and to notice where, as social
philosophies, the first two failed. Stoicism failed because
it ignored some of the most potent factors in human
nature.   It attempted to realise a union of human
beings without taking into account the conditions of
time and circumstance, or the idiosyncrasies of individual or national character. "What," asks Professor

Caird[1], "is meant by a φιλανθρωπία that is not fertile in special affections to individual human beings, affections which adapt themselves to their special character and the special relations into which they are brought? And what is meant by an organic unity of mankind in a πολιτεία τοῦ κοσμοῦ, if the reason that is to bind them together be taken merely as a common element in the nature of each, which connects them in spite of their differences in other respects? A real community cannot be constituted except between those whose common nature shows itself just in their differences, and makes these very differences the means of binding them together and fitting each for a special office in the common life. But the logic of the Stoics will not carry them to this further step. Hence the idea of the organic unity of mankind remains abstract, or turns into a mere ideal which never can be realised."

St Paul never fell into this error. He had far too deep a knowledge of human nature. He did not start, as the Stoic philosopher was apt to start, with a purely theoretic ideal. He took the various types of human nature, the various national and racial characteristics as he found them, but he also found a power in Christianity by which the noblest idiosyncrasies, whether of the individual or the community (while retained in their essence), could be sanctified, and, when sanctified, made to minister to the good of the race. Later, I hope to show that St Paul, with his ideas of unity of purpose, and of development towards

---

[1] *The Evolution of Theology in the Greek Philosophers*, Vol. ii. p. 126.

that purpose, in the realisation of which the widest differences of function should minister, anticipated the thought[1] of Comte, *i.e.* "of the whole human race, past, present and future, as constituting a vast and eternal social unit, where different organs, individual and national, concur in their various modes and degrees in the evolution of humanity." Towards this conception, no doubt, the Stoic teaching (whether it came to St Paul from the intellectual atmosphere of Tarsus, or through the instruction of Gamaliel) ministered. But in itself Stoicism never rose to this conception.

I need not dwell upon the parallel failure of the later Judaism, which, like Stoicism, showed an imperfect appreciation of the true 'nature' of human nature. As we have already seen, when its ideals ceased to be, in the highest sense of the words, 'human' and 'natural,' then it ceased to deal with things as they are, and consequently it ceased to meet the needs of men as these must be met[2]. The old prophets of Israel never fell into this error. They may, with the exception of the second Isaiah, have had a comparatively

---

[1] Quoted in H. Sidgwick's *Miscellaneous Essays and Addresses*, p. 256.

[2] The 'failure' of Stoicism is an example of a truth I have again and again tried to urge in these pages, viz., that any philosophy, or religion, or system of government which offends against those eternal laws by which the welfare of both the individual and society is governed, or which is untrue to the ' real nature,' or deepest wants of human nature, is *bound* to fail. The destined failure of 'compulsory' Socialism, should such ever be attempted in an extreme form, will proceed from the same cause—the failure to take into consideration the *facts* of human nature.

narrow outlook—as far as anything approaching cosmopolitanism is concerned—but their international teaching, as far as it went, was eminently real, and never vanished into a vague, shadowy, and merely theoretic idealism. We shall find that here again in spirit St Paul was far nearer to them than to either the Stoic philosophers or to those Jewish teachers who were contemporary with himself.

B. AS A PHARISAIC JEW.

We have seen that St Paul was in a very real sense a 'citizen of the world'[1]—that he was at home, as much as any man of that age could be, among 'all sorts and conditions of men.' We have learnt how strongly he seems to have been influenced by both Greek and Roman ideas, but this truth must not blind us to the fact that he was born and brought up and educated as a Pharisaic Jew, that Jewish influences were the earliest to be felt by him, and that certain of these (if reinterpreted by the light of Christianity and suffused and revivified by its spirit) continued to the end to be the foundation of his faith and of his teaching[2].

[1] 1 Cor. ix. 19 ff.

[2] A. McGiffert, *Christianity in the Apostolic Age*, pp. 115 ff.: see also G. G. Findlay in Art. 'Paul the Apostle,' *Hastings' Bib. Dict.* Vol. iii. p. 698.

" Ce n'est point l'enfant de la ville de Tarse, c'est le pharisien de Jérusalem...qui explique l'apôtre des Gentils." (Sabatier, *L'Apôtre Paul*, 3rd edition, p. 29.) Edward Caird, *The Evolution of Religion*, ii. 205 ff.

Indeed it would be only the truth to say that no one takes us into the very heart of Judaism—whether it be that of the Old Testament, or that contemporaneous with his own youth—no one reveals to us the very spirit of Judaism, both in its weakness and its strength, —as does 'the Apostle of the Gentiles.' No one but a Jew could have taught and written as St Paul. The Epistle to the 'Romans' contains a gospel for the world, the First Epistle to the Corinthians and the Epistle to the Colossians may have been addressed to almost entirely Gentile hearers, but a very brief examination of any of the three Epistles would be sufficient to convince us that no one but a Jew could have composed it[1].

St Paul's mind was saturated not only with the Old Testament, but with the contents of contemporaneous Jewish thought. Thus his conceptions of God and man and of man's true relation to God and to his fellow man were first formed from these, and if we remember that after his conversion he did not cease to read, but that he re-read, in a different (and far brighter) light, these Old Testament books, we shall be fully justified in saying that to the end of his life St Paul's conception of these relationships continued to be most strongly influenced by the highest and deepest teaching of the Old Testament[2]. Thus while

[1] "In der Hauptsache bleibt aber die Bildung des Paulus die Bildung des Rabbinen. Er hat sie an der Quelle gesucht...die Tatsache, dass Paulus durch die rabbinische Schule gegangen ist, steht fest aus seinen Briefen ; zu deutlich zeigen sie die Spuren." (Prof. Wrede, *Paulus*, p. 7.)

[2] " Le Dieu de Paul est celui...des Prophètes. " (Sabatier, p. 32.)

"C'est de l'Ancien Testament que Paul tient les notions premières et fondamentales de son système." (Sabatier, *L'Apôtre Paul*, p. 32.)

we do not forget what St Paul owed to both Greece and Rome we assert that these were but modifying influences colouring and expanding a Jewish faith most firmly and consistently held.

If we consider St Paul's Christian teaching;—what was this but the true, the natural and logical development, of the teaching of the Old Testament? Had we questioned St Paul, after his conversion (or any other of the apostolic teachers), he would doubtless have told us that he, and those who believed with him, were the true successors of the Old Testament teachers, that they, and not their fellow-countrymen who refused Christianity, were in the natural and legitimate line of descent from Abraham, through Moses and Elijah, Amos, Isaiah and Malachi[1].

It was then upon a mind filled with Jewish conceptions of (1) the natures of God[2] and man—the fundamental materials for a study of psychology and ethics, and, so far as the nature and possibilities of the *socius* are concerned, of sociology; (2) the true relationships between God and man, and between man and his fellow man—the fundamental materials for a study of sociology, and of the nature and possibilities of the *ideal society*—it was upon a mind so furnished[3] that the ideas, the light and teaching and spirit, of

[1] Hort, *The Christian Ecclesia*, p. 11 (ref. to Acts xv. 16): also p. 43.

[2] On St Paul's 'doctrine of God,' see G. B..Stevens, *Theology of N.T.* pp. 376 ff. : also on the relation between God and man, *ibid.* pp. 378 ff. On his doctrine of 'man,' *ibid.* p. 338 ff. On St Paul's Psychology, see Art. ' Psychology ' in *Hastings' Bib. Dict.*

[3] " ...wir in den psychologischen Prämissen der Bekehrung Pauli zugleich die Wurzeln seines eigenthümlichen Evangeliums suchen." (Pfleiderer, *Paulinismus*, p. 4.)

Christianity came in the case of St Paul. Christianity
both modified and developed all these conceptions, but
it was upon an original, main *substratum* of Jewish
ideas that Christianity became active. For this reason,
if we are to understand St Paul's 'Social Teaching,' we
must examine what in all probability would be, and, as
far as we have evidence to prove, what were, his social
conceptions previous to his conversion. By his 'social
conceptions' I mean his conceptions of man's true
relationship and duty towards his fellows, of his powers
and faculties for fulfilling these, also of his social ideals,
of those conditions of society which he felt it his duty
to strive to realise[1]. To perform this task adequately
would involve a careful investigation and exposition
of the sociological conceptions, and of the social and
political ideals, of the Pharisaic Jews during the time
of St Paul's youth, including an examination into their
psychology and their ethics. For such a task I have
no space. But what these conceptions were we can to
some extent gather, from a study, first, of a single field
or group of ideas—those which may be included under
the term *Messianic*; and secondly, from a study of
certain passages in St Paul's own letters, because these
letters, being to some extent apologetic, are also intensely, if indirectly, autobiographical. Many passages
in them are descriptive of the history and development
of St Paul's own thoughts and ideas, and of the changes
wrought in these by Christianity. They are the history
of a conflict of thoughts in which, if we listen carefully,

---

[1] *e.g.* "Der Pharisäismus...postulirte aber für deren wirkliche
Ankunft" (der messianischen Heilzeit) "ein *gerechtes* Volk."
(Pfleiderer, *Paulinismus*, p. 12.)

we may hear two voices—the voice of the Pharisaic Jew, as well as the voice of the convinced Christian Teacher. By listening to arguments, often expressed only in order to be refuted, we may learn much of St Paul's former convictions[1].

---

[1] "On le voit, c'est un corps de doctrines complet, cohérent et systématique, que Saul s'est formé aux pieds de Gamaliel....L'histoire de la pensée de Paul...n'est pas autre chose que celle de la transformation progressive, sous l'influence du principe chrétien, de ce pharisaïsme théologique qui fut sa croyance première." (Sabatier, *L'Apôtre Paul,* p. 35.)

CHAPTER II.

THE MESSIANIC HOPE[1].

THE Messianic ideas and hopes of the Jews in the time of St Paul is a subject of which it is difficult to give an account which shall be at once adequate and succinct. I must enter upon it only just so far as these ideas may be regarded as having tended to form and influence St Paul's social ideas and ideals before and after his conversion.

In speaking either of Messianic ideas, or of the Messianic ideal, we must remember that these changed greatly from time to time. Every ideal or product of the imagination is conditioned by the knowledge, and by the present circumstances of its possessor. So the Messianic ideals of the Jews were influenced by their

---

[1] For this see especially Davidson, *O. T. Prophecy*, chapters xviii., xix., xx. ; Schürer, *The Jewish People in the Time of Christ*, E. T. Div. II. Vol. ii. pp. 126 ff. ; Art. 'Messiah' (by V. H. Stanton) in *Hastings' Bib. Dict.*; Art. 'Messiah' in *Enc. Biblica*, by E. Kautzsch and T. K. Cheyne (based on Robertson Smith); W. Boussett, *Die Religion des Judentums*, pp. 199 ff. Cf. also T. K. Cheyne, 'Jewish Religious Ideals' (Lecture iii.) in his *Jewish Religious Life after the Exile*.

condition and their experiences during different epochs
of their history. And actually during the same epoch
the conceptions were different in different social *strata*,
e.g. among the learned, and the populace. The ideas of
most people upon this subject are formed from reading
the New Testament, and from reading that apart from
any general knowledge of the age in which it was
written and also of the immediately preceding age.
Consequently their conceptions are not only concentrated upon, but are apt to be actually limited to, the
thought of a *personal* Messiah. But a more careful
study, and one made upon a broader basis, will show
that the idea of the Messianic *Society* must not be
neglected[1]: such a study will show that at times the
idea of the personal Messiah faded into the background[2],
if it was held at all, at any rate in the sense which we
usually attribute to the term. Then, again, we shall
find that as the so-called 'national' hopes and expec-
tations of the Jews grew less and less justifiable, say
during the Roman dominion, there arose in the minds
of thoughtful men a natural tendency to transfer, or
postpone the fulfilment of the Messianic hope into a far
distant, and *supra-mundane* future. The 'eschatological'
interpretation of Messianic prophecy became more and
more common[3]; and, in connection with this tendency,

---

[1] See an interesting passage in Cheyne, *Jewish Religious Life
after the Exile* (pp. 94–95); N.B. also, " The Messianic age being the
time of the Church's perfection, any element that enters into the life
of men, as an essential factor of it, may be idealised and made
prominent." Davidson, *O. T. Prophecy*, p. 315.

[2] Boussett, p. 209. Schürer, E. T. II. ii. 159.

[3] *Enc. Bib.* p. 354.

the idea of fulfilment through human[1], or even national
agency receded in favour of a future directly-divine[2],
i.e. a miraculous intervention[3], through which the
Messianic reign should be introduced and established.
Further, the qualification for participation in that reign
tended to become more and more one of strict obedience
to legal and ceremonial enactments[4],—to the law enlarged and interpreted by an ever-growing body of
traditional rules,—rather than an ethical one[5]. [An
instructive proof of this lies in the gradually changing
significance of the word 'righteousness' *i.e.* of its
Hebrew and Greek equivalents.]

If now we turn from St Paul's contemporaries, or
his immediate predecessors, to the great Prophets of
Israel, and in particular to those passages in their
writings which may be regarded as 'Messianic,' *i.e.*
which speak of the hope of a better, or even of a
glorious future, we shall find (i) that this future,
though ultimately due to the Divine ordering and to
Divine power, is yet to be *realised* through the people
and for the people; (ii) that if the outlook is much

[1] "Der Gedanke dass die Frommen etwa Gott bei der Errichtung
des Reiches helfen könnten, liegt der spätjudischen Frömmigkeit im
Ganzen recht fern." (Boussett, p. 203.)

[2] Seen in the rise of 'Apocalyptic' Literature.

[3] "Erwartete man von der Zukunft auch noch wunderbarere
und grössere Dinge von Gott." (Boussett, p. 210.)

[4] "Man eifert für das Gesetz, um dereinst des Lohnes theilhaftig
zu werden." (Schürer, p. 499.)

[5] "...von einem Hungern und Dürsten dieser Frommen nach
Gerechtigkeit finden wir gerade in dem Umkreis der speciell messianischen Litteratur herzlich wenig." Boussett, p. 229. (Yet he draws
attention to the exception of the *Psalms of Solomon*.)

more circumscribed than that of later Judaism, it is
much more *natural*; and (iii) that the hope of its
realisation depends very much more upon an *ethical*
change in the character, and so in the conduct of
the people. These three features of earlier Messianic
prophecy are evidently closely related. For just as
Israel's misfortunes are by the Prophets always attributed to Israel's sins and unfaithfulness to Jehovah, so
if Israel's return to prosperity is to be 'mediated'
through the people (or through their human ruler as
the *representative* of the nation), an *ethical* change, a
return to the doing of Jehovah's will, is the natural
means through which this return to prosperity shall
be effected. A few examples may be very briefly
considered. Let us take (*a*) Is. ix. (2–7), (*b*) Is. xi.
1–8, (*c*) Ezek. xxxiv. 23, 24, (*d*) Ezek. xxxvii. 24, 25,
(*e*) Jer. xxiii. 5, 6, (*f*) Jer. xxxiii. 14–16. In every
one of these passages, or in the immediate context, the
ethical change which must precede, or accompany the
Messianic state is clearly asserted. In Is. ix. 7 we have
'to uphold it with judgement and with righteousness';
in Is. xi. 4, 'with righteousness shall he judge the poor,
and reprove with equity for the meek of the earth.'
In Ezek. xxxiv. the ethical conditions are stated in the
first verses of the chapter; immediately preceding the
promise in Ezek. xxxvii. we read, 'neither shall they
defile themselves...with any of their transgressions'...'all
their dwelling places wherein they have sinned.' And
in both passages from Jeremiah the ethical character
of Messiah's rule is made specially prominent. Again,
though in all these passages the figure of a personal
Messiah enters, he is in each a *human* figure, though

filled with the spirit of God; and neither in his
establishment nor in his rule have we anything
approaching a miraculous, divine intervention in the
ordinary sense of the term. In the first four passages
we have no mention of a king; in the last two the
second David is only to be chief or 'prince.' Then the
'everlasting covenant' is not with him personally, but
with him and his descendants as representing, and for
the benefit of, the people.

The passage in Is. lv. 3 ff. is conceived in the same
spirit, and here it is abundantly clear that the everlasting
covenant is not with any individual, but with the people
of Zion. The idea of a royal personality 'has lost
actuality'; each Israelite is a prince and the 'church-
nation' is Jehovah's anointed. Also in this passage
(v. 7) the conditions of blessing and of enjoyment are
distinctly ethical.

As we pass out of the period which may be termed
that of the Prophets more than one change comes over
the Messianic hopes and ideas. Possibly, now, Persian
influences colour these hopes, or at least the forms in
which they are expressed. Apocalypse takes the place
of Prophecy. The realisation of hopes is relegated to
a more distant and uncertain future, and the means
whereby this realisation is to be effected are more
supernatural[1]. Then a new conception of righteousness
is growing. 'Righteousness' is still the condition of
blessedness, but righteousness is becoming much more
obedience to the details of a legal code ever growing

---

[1] "Der diesseitige Charakter der alten Hoffnungen verschwindet
und ein jenseitiger, transcendenter macht sich stärker und stärker
bemerkbar." (Boussett, p. 198.)

in the minuteness of its requirements, it is even a
matter of strict observance of ceremonial regulations;
and 'blessedness' is being regarded more and more
as a condition only to be realised in some future life.
The growing belief in a resurrection is having a stronger
and stronger influence. In the well-known passage in
the Book of Daniel[1] the 'one like unto a Son of Man'
is, as Professor Driver shows, to be explained by 'the
saints of the Most High.' We have here no personal
Messiah. The realisation of the hope lies entirely
between God Himself and the ideal people. The hope
is realised by direct divine intervention; the whole
conception is eschatological, and has passed out of the
sphere of human and natural operation. As indicating
the interpretation put upon this passage by the Jews in
the first century B.C., we may refer to the 39th chapter
of the Book of Enoch, where the eschatological features
of the vision are much heightened.

Under the Roman dominion the wiser spirits among
the people saw less and less hope of any national
independence, at any rate of one capable of realisation
in the immediate future, and under present, *i.e.* mundane,
conditions[2]. But among 'the people' (the uneducated),
the tendencies towards attempting a 'national' uprising
and the hope of success in the same never entirely
died out. Indications of this difference of opinion are
found in the Gospels[3]. Among the educated (*e.g.* the
Pharisees) we see a not uncommon phenomenon in
religion—the contemporaneous development of apparently opposite ideas which ultimately meet. First, we

---

[1] vii. 12.   [2] Bousset, p. 196.
[3] *e.g.* St John xi. 48.

have the crystallization of 'Nationalism'; the Jew
becomes more a Jew[1]. He is sure that the future
belongs to him, but only so far as he proves himself
worthy to occupy the position which must be that of
the ideal people hereafter. Hence in the present he
falls back upon, and devotes himself to maintaining
by the strictest legal observances, the purity and
separateness of the Ideal Israel. Secondly, at the
same time as the realisation of his hopes fades even
still further into the future and the supra-mundane,
the ideas of Divine intervention and universal dominion
grow stronger. Coincidently with these tendencies
there vanishes from the minds of the educated any
idea, or even hope of a personal, human, and national
Messiah.

This short historical retrospect seems at least to
suggest :—

(i) That if we study the cycle of thought
in the midst of which St Paul was brought up, and
then consider his teaching, as found in his Epistles,
we can see how many of these contemporary Jewish
ideas were carried over into Christianity. We learn
the source of many ideas which henceforth found a
place in the Christian system, but which are either
unknown to the Gospels, or, if found there, may be
attributed to 'Pauline' or similar influences[2].

[1] The growth of the sentiment of ' Nationalism ' amid a widening
knowledge of, and an enlarged intercourse with other nations is an
interesting feature of the present age.

[2] "Denn nicht die Verschmelzung von Hellenismus und Judentum,
sondern die Eroberung beider für Jesus ist seine weltgeschichtliche
That." (Wernle, *Die Anfänge*, p. 134.)

(ii) That whenever St Paul looks forward to the
gradual realisation of a more perfect (social) state on
earth, and to this realisation as effected humanly and
naturally by means of a divinely inspired and guided
society, he is then going back, beyond the teaching of
his contemporaries and immediate predecessors, to that
of the Prophets. His conception of the Messianic
society, so far as it either is realised, or is to be
realised, under present human conceptions, finds its
antitype, not in the ideals of his own age, but in those
of the pre-exilic, and exilic Prophets. It was, I believe,
in a re-reading of their writings in a new light that his
ideas of what the Christian 'community-life,' and of
the fulfilment of its various relationships should be;
in short, it was by a study of these that his social
ideals were largely formed[1].

As examples of conceptions or ideas, affecting his
social teaching, which St Paul may be said to have
carried over from Judaism the following may be
given:—

(i) The perfect righteousness of God, and the
need of 'righteousness' in man, if man is to please
God and to do his duty to his fellow man, if he is to
realise, or fulfil the life for which God created and
destined him.

[1] The following combination of thoughts is interesting :

(1) " Paulus...was einer jener pharisäischen Schriftgelehrten, die
Jesu Wehe traf..." (Wernle, *Die Anfänge*, p. 96.)

(2) " Die Propheten sind die Erzieher Israels. Und diesen Beruf
übernahmen die Schriftgelehrten." (*Die jüdische Schriftgelehrsam-
keit*, Oscar Holtzmann.) See this pamphlet for a very interesting
discussion on the Scribes as the *successors* of the Prophets, and the
opposition of *both* to the Priests.

(ii)   The ideas connected with the conception
of a covenant people, a people who stand in a special
relationship with God, who somehow are to be the
means whereby the world is to be brought into
submission[1], or right-relationship to God, who are
ultimately to rule the world, but only under God as
their invisible King, and under One whom God might
appoint as His representative.

(iii)   The idea of a divine intervention on behalf
of man, and one supernatural in both the means and
manner in which it should be accomplished.

(iv)   Not only a whole circle of ideas which
might be gathered up under the single expression
'a knowledge of the Old Testament,' but also the use
of certain methods of interpretation of these Scriptures
—the methods of Halachah, Haggadah, and Sodh,
examples of each of which are to be found in St Paul's
Epistles[2].

By St Paul's 'Conversion' all these ideas (or the
ideas in each of these groups) were modified or transformed.   In some cases the transformation seems at
once to have been great, in others we can watch a
gradual transformation taking place during the course

---

[1] As an example of St Paul's practical aim see Ramsay, *Letters to
the Seven Churches*, p. 135.

[2] See R. L. Ottley, *Aspects of the Old Testament*, pp. 383 ff.
Where it is shown that St Paul inclines more particularly "to the
method of *Halachah* (the exegetical expansion of the Law) with free
use of allegorism," *e.g.* Rom. iv. 3–6, 1 Tim. v. 18; cf. Rom. iii. 10.
Of examples of *Haggadah*, we have the Messianic citations : of *Sodh*,
Ottley adduces 1 Cor. x. 1 ff., Gal. iv. 22 ff.

of his Christian teaching. Among such transformations
we may notice :—

(i) A different conception of the meaning of
righteousness[1]; of its 'mediate' source (the righteousness of man); and of the means whereby man becomes
a possessor of it. Also a much enlarged view of its
significance as a relation between man and man[2], while
retaining its significance of being the right relationship
between man and God.

(ii) A different conception of the relation of a
'covenant' people to the rest of the world; originally
the predominant idea was that of their privileges, now
it is that of their responsibilities. Any advantage
which they possessed was not to be regarded as a
privilege separating them permanently from the rest
of the world, but as a power to enable them to bring
the rest of the world into a position similar to their
own[3].

(iii) A very different conception of the *mode*
of the Divine 'intervention' for the good of men.
This difference of conception may be attributed to
a connection between (1) his enlarged knowledge of,
or his different conception of, the life and death of
Jesus, and of the ideals of Christianity, (2) a deeper
knowledge of the nature and needs of the human
'heart' (in the comprehensive Old Testament sense

---

[1] Sanday and Headlam, *Romans*, pp. 34 ff. Rom. x. 3.

[2] Rom. iii. 22.

[3] How St Paul may have gained this from a re-reading of the
'Servant' passages see Cheyne, *Jewish Religious Life after the
Exile*, pp. 88 ff.

of the word)[1]. This connection would modify his view
of both the essential nature of righteousness and of the
conditions necessary for righteousness.

(iv) An immense change in his 'reading,' *i.e.*
in his interpretation of the contents of the Old
Testament. This change was closely connected with
an alteration of view as to the relative importance
of different parts of the Canon. The Prophets and
the Law have changed places, and now the Psalms[2]
occupy a very important position.

[1] Driver on לְבָב (*Deut.* pp. 73, 74).

[2] There are at least twenty quotations from the Pss. in the Ep. to
the Romans alone.

CHAPTER III.

THE ISSUES OF THE 'CONVERSION.'

HAVING briefly indicated the chief sources of St Paul's ideas previous to his 'conversion,' we can now form some conception of the 'contents of his consciousness,' when certain Christian ideas took such hold upon him that they became, and continued to be, the dominant or overmastering motive powers of his life. By this consideration of the past we have to some extent equipped ourselves to see for what particular Christian ideas an entrance into his mind had been specially prepared, and for what particular development of certain of these ideas his previous knowledge and experience had made him an eminently suitable instrument.

We need not enter at length into the debatable question whether St Paul's submission to, or acceptance of, Christianity was gradual or sudden[1]. There is a *process* of victory as well as a *moment* of victory. Two sets of intellectual or spiritual forces may for a long period be at war within a man's heart. Still it is probably safe to say that, generally speaking, there is some psychological moment[2] at which the one set of

---

[1] See G. B. Stevens, *Theology of N.T.* pp. 327 ff.

[2] C. Gore, *Romans*, i. p. 264.

forces becomes so much the stronger that these now become, collectively, the ruling power of the life. But the new or victorious forces will, while ruling the old, continue to be still affected by these. The new will still be conditioned by the old; the old will be used by the new; and so the old will, to some extent, govern the direction of advance in the new life. A victorious general does not, when victory is assured, proceed to annihilate those he has subjected; they become tributaries, but his actions are still, to some degree, governed by their nature and capabilities.

We have, of course, three accounts of St Paul's conversion in the 'Acts,' viz. Acts ix. 1–30, Acts xxii. 3–21, Acts xxvi. 4–23. In his Epistles we have the passages in Rom. vii. 7–25, and Gal. i. 11–17, (besides many other indirect allusions) in which he alludes to the great change in his life; but for our present purpose we may confine our attention to the five passages here indicated. Even a brief examination of these passages will reveal one great difference between the three in the 'Acts' and the two in the Epistles. The former may be said to lay stress upon a psychological moment[1]; the latter seem at least to allow for a psychological process[2]. But a reconciliation is not impossible if we say that the former describe chiefly a certain critical moment, that of assured victory, in the course of a prolonged and intense struggle. And

---

[1] Yet see Acts xxvi. 14. Where there is the suggestion of struggling against an already, possibly for some time existing, opposing force.

[2] "St Paul has depicted the conflict in his pre-Christian life in Rom. vii. 7–25." (Stevens, *Theology of the New Testament*, p. 328.) See also C. Gore, *Romans*, i. pp. 260 ff.

when we read all these passages together (noticing carefully the various details in the sum of the evidence), we then obtain a remarkably full body of information, both as to the process and as to the great final conviction, which led to the change in the manner of the life. But we obtain more than this; we gain an insight into the means and process by which the old life passed into the new; and we see how closely connected these were. Taking the first three accounts, the critical moment is that in which St Paul becomes convinced that 'Jesus' is alive and in heaven; the result of which conviction is the further conviction that Jesus is 'the Messiah.' At once a new conviction has penetrated into St Paul's consciousness, humanly speaking by the aid of the whole group of Messianic ideas already within his consciousness; this conviction has attached itself to those previous ideas and will proceed to modify, or rather *transform* them. Only when we remember this identification of Jesus with the Messiah do we enter into the full significance of various current technical Messianic phrases in these three accounts, *e.g.* 'The Lord, even Jesus[1],' ix. 17; 'filled with the Holy Ghost,' ix. 17 (cf. Is. xi.); 'that he is the Son of God,' ix. 20; 'The Righteous One,' xxii. 14; 'be baptized[2],' xxii. 16; 'the hope of the promise made of God unto our fathers[3],' xxvi. 6.

[1] Note the identification.

[2] On the significance of baptism to a Jew, see Edersheim, *Life and Times of Jesus the Messiah*, i. pp. 273 ff. As the Israelites were bathed (Ex. xix. 10, 14) before entering into the covenant with God, so baptism would have the significance of entering into the New (Messianic) Covenant; see also Schürer, E. T. ii. ii. 319 ff.

[3] The Messianic Promise.

Now, in prosecution of my special purpose, I wish
to go a step further. But first I am prepared to admit,
even to affirm, that in all probability the meaning of
many phrases used by St Paul in the various accounts
of his conversion must be interpreted, not only in the
light of his previous Jewish training, but in the light
of the enlarged and deepened *Christian* experience
which he had gained *since* that event took place. To
those who read much autobiography the phenomenon
of a man almost unconsciously describing earlier
experiences in the light of later experience is by no
means an uncommon one. We need not assume that
when St Paul first became convinced of the Messiahship of Jesus, that he then saw either the consequences
or the possibilities[1] of this identification as he did when
he described his conversion to Festus and Agrippa, or
when he wrote his Epistles to the Ephesians and the
Colossians.

We must notice that in each account in the Acts
St Paul is described as (1) convinced of a fact,
(2) called to the promulgation of a truth, this latter
being a definite work or purpose within a definite
sphere. The truth was 'Jesus is the Messiah,' the
work or purpose being the promulgation of this truth
among the Gentiles[2]. I would here cite Dr Westcott's
dictum that every doctrine (or truth) is, (1) a fruit
of history, or experience, (2) a motive and guide, or
an inspiring, and regulating power of life and conduct.

---

[1] Stevens, *Theology of the N.T.* p. 330.

[2] Acts xxii. 21 (cf. Acts xiii. 47) and note that the 'commission'
is that to the 'Servant of the Lord' in Is. xlix. 6. [St Paul's work
is at once identified with that of 'the Servant.']

Thus every great truth or conviction, which issues at least partly from a reading of past history and experience, *e.g.* such a truth as 'Jesus is the Messiah,' carries with it certain consequences both intellectual and practical.

I here assume:—

(1) That no single truth, and especially no truth of religion, can be isolated. It is just a fragment of, and a living fragment, bound by ties of life to the great sum of all truth.

(2) That no truth, and again especially no truth of religion, can be divorced from life; its acceptance (or denial) must, for good or evil, consciously or unconsciously, affect life.

(3) That when we speak of anyone being convinced that 'Jesus is the Messiah,' the nature of the conviction, or the meaning of the expression, as well as the probable effects of the conviction, will vary according to both the contents of the knowledge, and the character of the person, being so convinced[1].

As no truth can be isolated, one truth or conception or idea (*e.g.* possibility of a truth) inevitably leads to another. For example, when St Paul became convinced that Jesus was the Messiah, then, in the light of the experience of 'Jesus,' the further truth of the possibility of a *suffering* Messiah must be admitted. But a suffering, divinely-appointed instrument for the good of God's people must, to one who knew the Old Testament, have suggested a further study of Is. liii.

---

[1] Also the subsequent effects will depend upon the use of the truth or truths primarily made.

which could not fail to be remembered in this connection. But this passage is only one of a group of
passages in the second Isaiah referring to the Divine
Servant, and must be read in close connection with
them. In this passage the suffering servant certainly
appears to be conceived as an individual, but he is
evidently a *representative* individual, who concentrates
in himself and personifies the sufferings of the *society* of
God's faithful servants; and such a society or company
never failed in Israel[1]. This representative individual
dies and rises again, and receives from God his vindica-
tion. And the effects of the death of this typical one, of
this preeminent example of the true Israel within Israel,
do not end with himself[2]. Here we see the possibility
of a further connection in St Paul's mind—that of the
sufferings and Messiahship of Jesus with a society of
which He is the head, among whom He is preeminent,
and in which His experiences will be repeated. Thus
the thought of the necessity of his own participation in
the sufferings of (the) Christ is revealed to St Paul
from the day when he recognised the Messiahship of
Jesus (Acts ix. 16). This last thought is much further
developed in the well-known passage in Col. i. 24[3],
where St Paul particularly associates his own personal
sufferings with those sufferings which are characteristic of membership in the Christian body[4] and
of participation in its work.

---

[1] Is. liii. 7, 10.

[2] Is. liii. 10 ff. וְתֵחָפֵץ יְהֹוָה בְּיָדוֹ יִצְלָח | יִרְאֶה זֶרַע | etc.

[3] N.B. ἀνταναπληρῶ τὰ ὑστερήματα τῶν θλίψεων τοῦ χριστοῦ...ὅ
ἐστιν ἡ ἐκκλησία.

[4] τοῦ χριστοῦ = an adjective.

C.   4

There is another circle of ideas which is very prominent in the narratives of the 'conversion,' and that is the references to *prophecy*. This is especially apparent in Acts xxvi. 16–18, where we have at least reminiscences of no less than six passages of Isaiah, two of Jeremiah, and one of Ezekiel[1]. And let us not forget that this passage contains St Paul's commission *from Messiah Himself*. The same is true of his account of the great change in his life which he gives us in Gal. i. 15[2].

Thus we see St Paul, from the very day of his conversion, going, with the conviction of the highest authority for so doing, to the Prophets for his inspiration to his mission. How far we have evidence for the *continuance* of this inspiration from the Prophets I hope to show later.

To us this may seem quite natural. But the Pharisee of St Paul's day did not attach the same relative importance to the Prophets, either in study or in the ministrations of religion, which we have learnt to do. To the Pharisee the Law was the essence or kernel of Holy Scripture, the rest—even the Prophets and Psalms—were only 'Commentary.' In the Synagogue, it appears, that from the Prophets only one lesson was read on only one day in the course of the week[3].

We cannot assert definitely that it was the 'voices of the Prophets,' and what we believe to be a true interpretation of them, that led directly to St Paul's

---

[1] Is. ix. 2, xxix. 18, xxxii. 3, xxxv. 5, xlii. 7, 16; Jer. i. 8, 19, xv. 20; Ezek. ii. 1.

[2] Is. xlix. 1, 5; Jer. i. 5.

[3] Schürer, E.T. II. ii. p. 81.

conversion. But there can be no doubt that in a very true sense Christianity was a revival of 'prophetic' religion. John the Baptist and our Lord both filled the office of a prophet[1], and our Lord distinctly connects His mission with the fulfilment of Messianic hopes and conditions.

Then in the early chapters of the Acts, *e.g.* in the speeches of St Peter on the Day of Pentecost[2], and in Solomon's Porch[3], and especially towards the close of St Stephen's speech[4], there is a marked and frequent reference to the Prophets. St Paul, whom we may assume would be present during St Stephen's speech[5], must have noticed this appeal to the Prophets, and by it he may have been sent to a fresh study of these, hence the commission at the time of his conversion—a commission based upon the Prophets—may have entered into a mind quite recently prepared to assimilate further teaching from this source.

Following the conversion comes St Paul's visit to Arabia. If we may accept Bishop Lightfoot's view of St Paul's purpose and probable experiences during this visit[6], we may assume that " here he" not only " read the true meaning and power of the law," but he may have remembered that "here also Elijah, the typical prophet,

---

[1] St Luke iv. 16 ff.

[2] Acts ii. 17 ff.; Joel ii. 28–32 ; Is. xxxii. 15, xliv. 3 ; Ezek. xxxvi. 27; and in *v.* 40 ff., Is. liv. 13 (xliv. 3), lvii. 19, etc.

[3] Acts iii. 19 ; Is. xliii. 25, xliv. 22, and in *v.* 26 ; Ezek. iii. 19.

[4] Acts vii. 42 ff.; Amos v. 25–27 ; Is. lxvi. 1, 2, etc.

[5] Sabatier, *L'Apôtre Paul*, p. 27. Bishop Gore, *Romans*, ii. p. 65, shows how in Rom. xi. we have an echo of St Stephen's argument.

[6] *Galatians*, p. 89.

listened to the voice of God, and sped forth refreshed
on his mission of righteousness"; in the haunts of the
greatest of Old Testament Prophets St Paul may have
re-studied the teaching of the Prophets, and may from
them have learnt " the breadth as well as the depth of
the riches of God's wisdom[1]."

Then in one of the earliest of his recorded speeches
St Paul ascribes the persecution and death of our Lord
by the Jewish rulers to their ignorance of ' the voices
of the prophets[2],' which at the same time, as he shows,
they had unconsciously fulfilled; and St Paul's warning
to his hearers, lest they should copy this evil example,
is taken directly from the prophecies of Habakkuk[3],
and Isaiah[4], and when the Jews actually did refuse his
mission, and he turned to the Gentiles, it is by an
appeal to the second Isaiah that he justifies this action[5].

---

[1] See also Stevens, *Theology of the N.T.* p. 331.

Sabatier on St Stephen's speech (*L'Apôtre Paul*, p. 21), "il
découvre sans ménagement la cause secrète de cette opposition
invincible que les juifs ont toujours faite à la parole des Prophètes."

[2] Acts xiii. 27 (ἀγνοήσαντες has at least the suspicion of 'culpable'
ignorance).

[3] i. 5.   [4] xxix. 14.

[5] Is. xlix. 6 (xlv. 22) ; see also xlii. 6.

CHAPTER IV.

THE USE OF THE OLD TESTAMENT PROPHETS IN ST PAUL'S EPISTLES.

I NOW turn to St Paul's use of the Prophets in his Epistles, and while I have no wish to lay stress upon the mere number of quotations in these from the Prophets, still the comparative frequency with which certain books are referred to in support of an argument is at least some indication of the writer's sense of their importance and their usefulness, and especially for that purpose[1]. Space will not permit me to examine all the quotations from the Prophets in all the Epistles, I propose therefore in the first place to draw attention to those found in the Epistle to the Romans, the Epistles to the Corinthians, and the Epistle to the Ephesians.

At the end of Westcott and Hort's edition of the Greek Testament is found a list of quotations from the Old Testament in the New. From this list I find there

---

[1] "There are many points in which the teaching of St Paul bears a striking resemblance to that of the old Prophets. It is not by chance that so many quotations from them occur in his writings" (Sanday and Headlam, *Romans*, p. 305): see the whole of the Additional Note (pp. 302 ff.) on 'St Paul's Use of the Old Testament.'

are 87 such quotations in the Epistle to the Romans, of which 32 are from the Prophets, 21 from the Psalms, and 24 from the five books of the Law; but of these 24 no less than 13 are references to the history of the patriarchs, and 4 are from the Ten Commandments. In the First Epistle to the Corinthians there are 31 quotations from the Old Testament of which 15 are from the Prophets. In the Second Epistle to the Corinthians out of 31 quotations 14 are from the Prophets, and of 30 quotations in Ephesians 16 are from the Prophets.

The nature of the quotations in the writings of any author and the sources from which they are taken will, of course, as I have just stated, be largely governed by his subject and by the nature of his arguments; but I think these figures may be regarded as showing that St Paul was not only very familiar with the Prophets, but that he regarded their teaching as of very great importance.

Now, taking these same four Epistles, we have in them together 77 quotations from the Prophets, of which no less than 32 are from the second part of the Book of the Prophet Isaiah. From this I think we may infer that this Prophet (or this collection of prophecies) had either a special attraction for, or a special influence upon St Paul.

Once more; we shall find, if we examine them, that a very considerable proportion of these 32 quotations are taken from what are now generally termed the 'Servant' passages in that collection of prophecies. Hence I conclude that St Paul must have been specially impressed with the teaching contained in these passages, and with its peculiar applicability to the

IV]

particular purpose to which his life was now devoted—the exposition of Jesus as the Messiah[1].

I would now approach the subject from a slightly different point of view. No one who has studied the Prophets of the Old Testament will, I think, contravene these two statements:—

(1) That the Prophets are the great teachers and preachers of *righteousness*.

(2) That this righteousness is, from the time that Elijah appears as the champion of Naboth, very largely a *social* righteousness[2]; in other words, the Prophets demand not only a right relationship towards God, but a right relationship *between men*.

It is almost unnecessary to cite examples to prove these statements. The evils from which the Prophets saw the people suffering were largely due to the want of this righteousness, and the welfare of the people, if it was to be restored and maintained, implied a return to, and a practice of righteousness.

When we pass from the atmosphere, the teaching, the ideals of the Prophets to those of the later Jews, *e.g.* those of the Pharisees, it is not that righteousness is no longer the ideal,—it is rather that the *conception* of righteousness has changed; it has become im-

[1] Also of Jesus as the Servant of the Lord. But also of the Christian Society as the 'social' servant.

[2] "In condemning the murder of Naboth Elijah pleaded the cause of Jehovah as the cause of civil order and righteousness....The Sovereignty of Jehovah was the refuge of the oppressed, the support of the weak against the mighty." (Robertson Smith, *The Prophets of Israel*, p. 87.)

poverished[1]. We feel this in all the accounts of every
dispute between our Lord and the Pharisees, and it is
especially on the social side of righteousness that this
impoverishment has taken place. The Pharisees have
a zeal towards God, but they do not realise that the
service of God cannot be fulfilled apart from the service
of man. And the service of man as conceived and
preached by the Old Testament Prophets is not confined
to the service of those who belong to some particular
nation[2], or to some particular class within the nation.
The ideals of the Prophets are expressed in such sayings
as "For the earth shall be full of the knowledge of the
Lord as the waters cover the sea," or "Unto me every
knee shall bow, every tongue shall swear." But the
precepts of the Pharisees were full of distinctions of
the treatment due to a *Chaber*, or to one of the
Am-harrez[3]. To the Pharisees there seem to have been
at least three classes, (1) themselves, (2) the bulk of
the people, (3) the heathen. And the distinction
between the first and the second was equally great
with that between the second and the third. To the
esoterically-minded Pharisee, the ideal of St Paul in
Col. i. 28 must have sounded almost blasphemous[4].

[1] See Art. 'Righteousness in N.T.' in *Hastings' B. D.* iv. p. 282
(by G. B. Stevens).

[2] N.B. Amos i. and ii.

[3] Schürer, E. T. II. ii. 24 ff.

[4] Next in magnitude to the change in St Paul's attitude towards
Christ came the change in his attitude towards ' man ' (before and
after his 'conversion'). Yet we can imagine a Pharisee of the
Diaspora as more prepared for this new view of man than a
Palestinian Pharisee. On ' The Jews in Asian Cities,' see Ramsay's
Seven Churches, pp. 155 ff. ; cf. pp. 131 ff.

The Pharisee seems to have delighted in distinctions: yet such distinctions, whether national, intellectual, or spiritual, were fatal to a true view of either social life or social duty. They were totally opposed to the spirit of the Prophets[1]. A righteousness whose expression towards humanity was satisfied by honouring some and by despising others was not the righteousness of Amos, Hosea, or Isaiah.

[1] *e.g.* Is. xlix.

CHAPTER V.

A.

AN adequate examination of the influence of the teaching of the Prophets upon the Social Teaching of St Paul might demand a volume to itself. It would be a shorter task to show the influence of the second Isaiah upon the Apostle's teaching; but I propose to content myself now with an even narrower field of enquiry than this,—to try to show how many analogies there are between the ruling ideas of the so-called 'Servant' passages, and St Paul's social teaching. In tracing these analogies I do not propose to confine myself strictly to 'quotations' in St Paul's writings from these passages; I would rather try to show how the leading ideas of these passages are reproduced and developed by St Paul.

The following interpretation of these 'Servant' passages is, I think, now widely accepted. When the Prophet speaks of the 'Servant,' he is using, at any rate in the first instance, a term for 'Israel' which would not be wholly unfamiliar to the intelligent hearer. God had in the past chosen Israel for a mighty work—

a *service* to Himself. But the great mass of the people
had proved either deaf or unfaithful to this call, and
therefore to the realisation or fulfilment of this purpose
or service. Hence while the 'Servant' *should* mean
Israel as a *whole*, actually it means that fragment or
remnant of Israel which is *really* trying to live the
life which the people should live, and doing the work
which, as a whole, they should do.

Before considering whether the 'Servant' is an
individual or a society it may be well to notice the
following 'notes' or features of the Servant's Office and
Mission, and of the manner in which that Mission is
fulfilled.

(1) He is the anointed prophet of the Lord, Is. lx. 1[1].
(We must bear in mind all that the prophetic office
[and work] implies.)

(2) He is the representative of the 'new covenant'
between God and His people, Is. xlii. 6; cf. xlix. 8. [The
phrase is strange, but probably means that the prophet
or servant is the mediator or medium of the covenant
between God and Israel.]

---

[1] Is Isaiah lxi. 1 ff. a 'Servant' passage? (1) Skinner (*in loc.*) thinks
the objections against are the stronger. (2) Cheyne (*Isaiah*, ii. p. 93),
on the whole, thinks 'yes' for *vv.* 1–3. "This need not hinder us
from admitting that *vv.* 4–9 have nothing to mark them out as
belonging to the 'Servant.'" (3) G. A. Smith is undecided, but says:
"On the whole there is less objection to its being the Prophet who
speaks than the Servant" (*Isaiah*, ii. p. 435). [Also see list of
authorities *for* and *against* given in his note.] (4) Davidson, *O. T.
Theology* (p. 263): "After chap. liii. the servant does not appear
except perhaps in lxi. 1–3." (5) Driver, *Introduction to O.T.* (p. 222):
"In lxi. Jehovah's ideal servant is once more introduced." See also
Cheyne, *Jewish Religious Life after the Exile*, p. 92.

(3)   The mission of the Servant is not confined to
Israel after the flesh: he realises that it is world-wide in
scope, Is. xlix. 6; cp. xlii. 6.   [It must be remembered
that it was in these words that St Paul received his
great commission—as an apostle to the Gentiles; a
charge received under such circumstances (*i.e.* of the
conversion) might well be branded into his memory.
Might it not also lead him to connect his own work,
and that of those associated with him, with the work
of the Servant of the Lord?]

(4)   The manner (or spirit) in which the Servant
fulfils his mission, Is. lxi. 1 ff.   The keynote of the
method and spirit of the Christian mission was at once
struck when our Lord appropriated to Himself these
well-known words[1].   The gentleness and tenderness of
the method by which the mission is to be fulfilled is
noticed by St Paul, 2 Cor. x. 1[2].

(5)   The Servant's work is one which can only be
fulfilled and accomplished through suffering, Is. liii.
This was directly foretold to St Paul at the time of
his conversion and immediately after the words taken
from the 'Servant' passage.   St Paul distinctly recog-
nises this in a very striking passage, Col. i. 24[3].

[1] St Luke iv. 16 ff.

[2] I must not anticipate, but I may note that here we have τοῦ
χριστοῦ, the meekness and gentleness which is characteristic of the
Messianic work, society, spirit, etc.

[3] The following sentences from Prof. Cheyne, *Jewish Religious Life
after the Exile*, p. 217, suggest some interesting parallels between 'the
Servant' and St Paul and his work : "...the exquisite poems on the
Servant of Jehovah...represent a perfect fusion of the legal and the
prophetic religion.   The Servant of Jehovah, *i.e.* the company of
religious teachers...was to convert first lukewarm or indifferent

B.

I now wish to sketch very briefly an argument for which in its main features I am especially indebted to Professor G. A. Smith (*Isaiah*, Vol. ii.) and to the late Professor A. B. Davidson (*Old Testament Prophecy*). Professor Smith points out that when 'the Servant' is first introduced (in xli. 8) the title is clearly a designation of the whole "historical nation, descended from Abraham[1]," this is clear from the parallel, "seed of Abraham." We seem to have a similar conception in xliv. 1 ff. and xliv. 20, where the 'Servant' is called both 'Jacob' and 'Israel'—the national names.

But the nation as a whole did not realise the idea. The people were 'sifted by the call,' or summons to the Divine Mission and in xlii. 6, "I the LORD...will keep thee and give thee for a covenant of the *people*[2],

Jews, and then the other nations, to the true religion. The spirit of his preaching was prophetic....It is an everlasting covenant which a late prophet declares that the earth's inhabitants have broken...he is well assured that the neglect of the simple precept of respect for human life will bring the wrath of God upon the offending nations." (Cp. St Paul's picture of the Gospel and the Gentile world in Romans i.)

Cf. 2 Cor. i. 5, where we have twice (according to the correct reading) τοῦ χριστοῦ. [This is one of the many passages in which ὁ χριστός may have much more than a personal significance.]

[1] p. 256.

[2] עַם (sing.).

A reference to xlix. 8 shows that Israel is meant. 'A covenant for the people,' because the Servant of Jehovah, who so thoroughly

for a light of the Gentiles," we have a conception of
the 'Servant' which is clearly not that of the *whole*
people. The phrase 'a covenant of the people' is both
difficult and suggestive. (It occurs again in xlix. 8.)
But it is probably to be explained, in accordance with
the parallel phrase, 'a light of the Gentiles,' as referring
to that section of the people who were faithful to the
Divine call, and who should be a mediator¹ of a covenant
between Jehovah and Israel. Then in xlix. 3, 6 (where
we have the Servant's testimony to Himself) the Servant
claims the title of Israel, yet here again he is evidently
not the whole nation, as his task is 'to bring Jacob
again' to Jehovah. Here "the prophet speaks out of
the heart of the Servant, in the name of that better
portion of Israel, which was already conscious of the
Divine call, and of its distinction in this respect from
the mass of the people²."

In the important passage l. 4–10 the term 'Israel'
is not found; here the conception of the 'Servant' does
not seem to be that of even a part of the nation standing
over against the nation, but as if he were an individual
over against other individuals. The chief reason for

knows His will, and is empowered to carry it out, is like an embodiment of His promise or agreement (בְּרִית), cf. 2 Cor. iii. 2, 'Ye are
our epistle.' (Note by Cheyne, *Jewish Religious Life after the Exile*,
p. 92.)

¹ Thus one part of the Servant's work is the fulfilment of the
'mediatorial office.' This was the work of Christ : it is the work of
the Church—the Social Christ, 2 Cor. v. 18. Note also 2 Cor. iii. 6,
διακόνους καινῆς διαθήκης in connection with διὰ τοῦ χριστοῦ in *v.* 4
(through our position and commission in the society and work of
the Christ).

² G. A. Smith, *Isaiah*, ii. p. 265.

drawing special attention to these verses is that they seem to supply the transition from the social conceptions in the earlier 'Servant' passages to the well-known passage in lii. 13—liii. where, if anywhere, the conception of the 'Servant' is distinctly personal or individual.

In the following chapter Professor Smith proceeds to deal with 'the Servant of the Lord in the New Testament.' Before, however, considering any details let us remind ourselves that in a very real sense the entrance of Christianity into the world meant the revival of 'prophetism[1].' Both John the Baptist and our Lord are, as far as concerns the main features of their work, 'prophets.' One ideal of the Old Testament was expressed thus, 'would God that all the LORD'S people were prophets[2].' One ideal of New Testament religion is thus described, "Follow after love; yet desire earnestly spiritual gifts, but rather that ye may prophesy....I would have you all speak with tongues, but rather that ye should prophesy[3]." But Christianity was not only a revival of prophecy generally, it was a revival of the ideas—of the teaching, aspirations, and hopes—of the second Isaiah. Professor Smith says[4], "In the generation, from which Jesus sprang, there was, amid national circumstances closely resembling those in which the second Isaiah was written, a counterpart of that Israel within Israel which the prophet has

[1] See an interesting passage on the prophet as *mediator* in Davidson, *Old Testament Prophecy*, p. 5.

[2] Numb. xi. 29.   [3] 1 Cor. xii. 1 ff.

[4] *Isaiah*, ii. p. 281.

personified in ch. xlix. The holy nation lay again in bondage to the heathen, partly in its own land, partly scattered across the world; and Israel's righteousness, redemption, and ingathering were once more the questions of the day." As far as the political conditions were concerned there may have been some analogy between the position of the Jews in the sixth century B.C. and the first century A.D., but I think Professor Smith possibly pushes the similarity of religious aspiration too far, especially when he adds, "around the temple and in quiet recesses of the land, a number[1] of pious and ardent Israelites lived on the true milk of the word, and cherished for the nation hopes of a far more spiritual character. If the Pharisees laid their emphasis on the Law, this chosen Israel drew their inspiration rather from prophecy, and of all prophecy it was the Book of Isaiah, and chiefly the latter part of it, on which they lived. As we enter the Gospel History from the Old Testament, we feel at once that Isaiah is in the air." He then points out that in "the songs of the Nativity, and in the description of Simeon we have many echoes of the second Isaiah, and especially of the 'Servant' passages in the same[2]." Then he reminds us that "in the fragments of the Baptist's preaching, which are extant, it is remarkable that almost every metaphor and motive may be referred to the Book of Isaiah, and mostly its exilic half....Our Lord, then,

[1] I think Prof. Smith's language here may lead his readers to think that this 'number' was far larger than in all probability it actually was. The evidence for the statement appears to me only slight.

[2] p. 282.

sprang from a generation[1] of Israel, which had a
strong conscience of the national aspect of the Service
of God,—a generation with Isaiah xl.—lxvi. at its
heart."

All this may be true, but as we cannot determine
the "sources to which St Luke went for this part of
his Gospel,—a part be it remembered peculiar to his
Gospel,"—it seems to be somewhat unwise to assume
quite so much as Professor Smith would have us
assume[2]. What appears to be far more certain is that
our Lord (both in the letter and the spirit) claimed for
Himself much that was in close agreement with the
position and the teaching of the Servant of the Lord,
and especially as this culminates and passes out of view
in Is. liii.

Our Lord's work according to His own estimate of
it is 'service'[3] and especially 'social' service; and this
may be said to be His favourite conception of His
Mission. As we have already seen, He claims the
fulfilment of Isaiah lxi. ff. as His own work. His
favourite simile for portraying the Kingdom of Heaven
lies in the difference between willing and unwilling,
true and false, faithful and unfaithful, *service*[4]. He is
among those who have associated themselves with His

[1] This word being ambiguous in meaning (*time v.* nature) seems
unfortunate here, and here again I think that the number, or proportion, of the people which had the second Isaiah "at heart" was
probably far less than is assumed.

[2] The reader will not fail to notice that the 'echoes' of the second
Isaiah occur in the most 'Pauline' of the Gospels.

[3] St Matt. xx. 26 ff. ; St Mark x. 43 ff.; St Luke xxii. 27.

[4] St Matt. xviii. 23, xxiv. 45, xxv. 21; St Luke xii. 43, etc.

purpose "as one that serveth." With Him service is
the chief claim to respect and the secret and source
of influence[1].

When we pass from the Gospels to the Acts we find
that the title, and so the conception of our Lord as the
Divine 'Servant' was familiar to the early disciples,
e.g. Acts iii. 13, 26, iv. 27, 30, etc.

I now come to what I believe to be a very important step, or transition of thought, which must be
taken (or made) in any adequate attempt to form a
conception not only of St Paul's Social Teaching, but
of the Teaching of the New Testament generally—a
conception which will also help us to form a true
appreciation of the position of the Christian Church
in the world.

Briefly the conception is this, that as in' the
'Servant' passages in the Second Isaiah the conception
of the 'Divine Servant' *narrows down* from the *whole*
people to a *section* of the people, and then (apparently)
at last to a *representative Individual*; so in the New
Testament the conception of the 'Divine Servant'
broadens out (almost from the first) from the Representative Individual—our Lord, Who fulfils in Himself,
in His work, in His perfect Self-sacrifice, all the mani-
fold forms of Divine service—to the first circle of His
followers, the 'infant Ecclesia[2].' In the early chapters

---

[1] St Matt. xx. 27, xxiii. 11.

[2] "In the Old Testament the Messiah is the concentration of the
people ; in the New, the people are the extension of the Messiah. In
the Old, He had not come; the Church was pregnant with Him,

of the Acts we see this Society being gradually but constantly enlarged by the accession of new members; though St Paul seems to have been the first to grasp in all its fulness the meaning of the charge to "go into all the world and to preach the gospel to every creature," and, in virtue of this charge, to give his life to the task of making the Church or Ecclesia coextensive with the human race[1].

But as the Society grows it must not lose any of its essential or characteristic features. As its first members were united with, and represented their Master[2], so must *all* its members, however numerous these may be. He had combined Divine Service and Social Service; in the service of man He had rendered service to God, and every true follower of His, every member of His society, must do the same. Thus ultimately the conception of the Divine Servant (for

ready to bring forth the man child; in the New, He is the firstborn, the head of all." (Davidson, *O. T. Prophecy*, p. 343.)

On "The Church" as "the extension and perpetuation of the Incarnation in the world," see C. Gore, *Bampton Lectures*, p. 219 f.

[1] Hort, *Christian Ecclesia*, p. 148.

[2] There can be no doubt that the first disciples considered that the object of the Christian Society was to represent Christ, to continue His work, through and in His Spirit, and according to His methods. It is hardly necessary to give proofs of this; they are everywhere in the early chapters of the Acts. The disciples are Christ's witnesses (Acts ii. 32). In His Name the Apostles teach and heal (Acts iii. 6), that is they perform His two most characteristic works; upon the ground of His Name, the early converts are baptised (Acts ii. 38). It is also at least possible that the so-called 'communism' of the first days may have been an attempt to perpetuate the custom of the common purse of Christ and the twelve.

St Paul[1] regarded the Christian Church as a single
organism with a single life and purpose) expands and
rises, not only to the Old Testament conception, but far
beyond it. It is by St Paul regarded as coextensive
with the Israel of God[2], but this Israel is meant to be
ultimately coextensive with the human race.

But there is another thought which must be most
carefully connected with this expansion, if its full
significance (its continuity with the old, and its meaning to St Paul in particular) is to be understood. We
must remember that the early chapters of the Acts are
full of Messianic references. The long quotation from
Joel[3] in St Peter's speech upon the Day of Pentecost
has a Messianic significance. The exhortation at the
close of the same speech is based upon the claim for
Jesus of the Messiahship[4], and for those who accept
Him as such a share in the Messianic promise. The
baptism of the converts which immediately follows "is
the definite act which signifies at once their faith in
Jesus as Messiah...and the acceptance of them by
the Ecclesia[5]." And this 'new Ecclesia' which was
claiming for itself the hope of Israel was not at first
"in any antagonism to the old Ecclesia but the most
living portion of it[6]." Again, in St Peter's speech
after the healing of the lame man, the Messiahship is
claimed for Jesus[7], and the result of the 'Servant's'
work (the work of Jesus, now carried on by His

---

[1] In the Ephes. Ep.   [2] Gal. vi. 16.
[3] Acts ii. 17–21.   [4] Acts ii. 31 (Ps. xvi. 16).
[5] Hort, *Christian Ecclesia*, p. 44.   [6] *Ibid.* p. 45.
[7] Acts iii. 20.

servants who represent Him) shall be blessing (a
Messianic phrase), in turning away men from their
iniquities.

The passage in Acts iv. 27–31 should be most carefully noticed. Here the Servantship and the Messiahship (ὃν ἔχρισας) of Jesus are united, and immediately
after comes the term 'thy servants' (τοῖς δούλοις σου[1])
of the members of the Church generally. And we
must note that they pray for power "to speak the
word…while Thou" (through them as in the case of
the lame man) "stretchest forth Thy hand to heal, and
that signs and wonders may be done through (διὰ) the
name of Thy Holy Servant[2] Jesus." Immediately the
prayer is followed by a gift of the Holy Ghost, in itself
a Messianic Blessing[3].

The importance of this passage for my present
purpose lies in its proof of the prevalence (at the time
it was written) of the closest possible connection of
certain ideas, viz. (1) The Messiahship of Jesus, (2) The
'Servantship of Jesus,' (3) That speaking the word,
signs and wonders, and healing—the characteristic
marks of the activity of Jesus—may continue, (4) That
the members of the Church are now Servants of the

---

[1] πρὸς τοὺς ἰδίους in v. 28.

[2] τοῦ ἀγίου παιδός σου 'Ιησοῦ. For the following note I am indebted
to Prof. G. A. Smith : " In Is. xl.–lxvi. the LXX translates the Heb.
(= always עֶבֶד) for Servant by either παις or δουλος : παις is used in
xli. 8, xlii. 1, xliv. 1ff., xliv. 21, xlv. 4, xlix. 6, l. 10, lii. 13, but δουλος
in xlviii. 20, xlix. 3, and 5.   In Acts it is παις that is used of Christ."
"An apostle is never called παις, but only δουλος Θεου" (Meyer).
David is called παις in Acts iv. 25.

[3] Is. xi. 1 ff.

LORD, and that all is done διὰ τοῦ ὀνόματος (as representatives of the office and as trustees of the power). I need not pursue this examination any further in order to show the existence among the first disciples of such ideas as (a) the Messiahship and Servantship of Jesus, (β) the Servantship of His followers, and their consciousness (if as yet dim) that their office (and task), not merely as individuals, but as members of the *Society* which He founded and which represents Him, was to be associated together and with Him in the *Messianic* work, and to aid in bringing about the *Messianic* state and reign.

But it was by St Paul that the possibilities of the amplification or development, and of the 'applicability' of these ideas were first recognised in anything approaching to completeness. What I now wish to urge is that St Paul's conception, not only of the ideal, but of the actual Christian Society, his conception of the ideal life *among* its members, and of its responsibilities "towards those which are without," can only be rightly understood when it is read not simply in the light of his great conviction—'Jesus is the Messiah'—but in the light *of the inevitable deductions or consequences* of that conviction, viz. that the Messiah is the 'Servant,' that the Christian Society is the true Messianic Society, that this Society is *only* an *extension* of the Messiah, and may be *identified* with Him, that this Society *is the Servant*, as well as a Society of Servants, and that the true conception and fulfilment of all social relationships and virtues and duties springs out of this conviction and these inevitable deductions.

And, further, we shall find that the ethical characteristics of the Messiah *are*, and so the ethical characteristics of the members of the Messianic Society *must
be*, the virtues exhibited in the human life of the
personal, or historic, Jesus[1]. We shall also find that
these are very largely the virtues of the 'Servant of
the Lord.' We have thus, indirectly, a very striking
corroboration of the Unity of the Old Testament and
the New, and that in a sphere where they are supposed
sometimes to be little in agreement; besides, we obtain
a valuable argument in the field of apologetics:—The
'truth of the Gospel' is found not to depend simply
upon evidence for certain historic events, but to lie
also in its wonderful truthfulness to human nature,
upon its insight into the needs and possibilities of that
nature, and especially upon its insight into its social
possibilities[2], the possibilities of man regarded as a
socius[3].

Our next task must be to consider the Messianic
ideas and Messianic teaching of St Paul during that
period of his life when he was active as a Christian
Teacher and Missionary.

I have already pointed out how it was the conviction that Jesus was the Messiah that ultimately
became the turning-point in St Paul's life: from a
consideration of his education and previous experience
I have also shown what ideas connected with the term

[1] See Additional Note, p. 75.

[2] See Additional Note on 'St Paul's Realism,' p. 142.

[3] For an explanation of this term and the ideas connected with it
see chapter vii. p. 93 ff.

Messiah we may with fairness conclude were in his consciousness previous to his conversion[1]. Now, from an examination of certain passages in his Epistles I would try to show what his 'Messianic' teaching actually was. Let us then consider St Paul in the very centre or height of his activity as a Christian Teacher and Missionary, say at the time when he wrote the Epistle to the Romans, or when he wrote the Epistle to the Ephesians.

We may assume that then he regarded the 'Christian' Society, which he was labouring to construct and enlarge, as the perfect or ideal society. And, like every great constructive teacher or worker, we may believe he had some vision of his object[2]. Towards the realisation of this vision he was devoting his life. This ideal society may be most briefly and comprehensively described by the single word 'Christian.' Now to St Paul the ideas conveyed by this word would be doubly descriptive. (1) It was simply a translation of 'Messianic.' (2) It must have meant 'according to the ideals and the will of Jesus.' Hence we have three terms which are absolutely synonymous. (a) 'Perfect[3].' (β) 'Messianic.' (γ) 'According to the Spirit and Teaching and Will of Jesus.' Each of these terms will serve equally well to describe the Society which, as I have just said, St Paul was

[1] I would particularly remind the reader of the idea of a Messianic ruler or leader ruling over a faithful body of followers or a Messianic people. [The combination of the ideas of the personal and social (or national) Messiah.]

[2] See quotations from the Epistle to the Ephesians in note on 'St Paul's Realism,' p. 142.

[3] Or 'Ideal.'

labouring to construct. Once more; until this Society was co-extensive with the human race, until every human being was perfect—according to the perfection of the Christian or Messianic standard,—the purpose and work of Jesus, the Christ, which was also the Divine purpose, could not be said to be 'fulfilled.'

To a Christian-Jew like St Paul the Divine purpose could not be regarded as commencing, or as entering into the world with the life and work of the human-personal Christ, the Jesus of history. The incarnation and human life of (the) Christ was only one step, if the greatest of all steps, in the fulfilment of the Divine purpose[1]. For previous to His birth there had been in the world for many generations a Divine Society; of this Society the incarnate personal Christ was in a true sense both a factor and a product. This Society had again and again, through the imperfections of its members, failed of its purpose. Still that purpose, because it was Divine, could not ultimately fail. The idea had been maintained, and the hope of its realisation, if under different forms in different periods, had continued or persisted.

In the historic personal Christ we have the first realisation of a perfect humanity, and one in which the social virtues are perfectly expressed; and from Him the Divine Society took a new start. If we contemplate the work which Jesus had accomplished at the time of His Ascension, we cannot regard His work as completed or His purpose fulfilled[2]. St Paul

---

[1] Ephes. iii. 9 ff.　　　　[2] Acts i. 1, ἤρξατο.

realised this. He, as a Christian-Jew, saw in Jesus
the Messiah, the long expected Messianic King or
Ruler; and he recognised that in the person of Jesus,
as far as personal realisation was possible, there had
been embodied and expressed the highest and most
spiritual ideals of the most spiritual prophets and
teachers of the past.

But, as we have already noticed, the spiritually
minded Jews, both of St Paul's own age and of the
ages preceding that, did not look forward only to a
personal Messiah[1]. If they regarded Messiah as
a King, He must have subjects, if as a Priest, he
would have fellow-worshippers, if as a Prophet, there
would be a widespread knowledge of the Divine Will.
The devout Jews looked forward to a Messianic State
or Society. Apart from a Society the Messianic hope
or purpose could not be fulfilled.

St Paul when he became a Christian must have
possessed this idea, he now gives it a Christian interpretation, indeed under the influence of Christianity
he enormously enlarges and expands it. He clearly
regards the work and the purpose of Jesus, the
Messiah, as yet incomplete. Even His sufferings were
incomplete[2]. His Messiahship is incomplete. The
Christian Society which Jesus founded, out of the old
Divine Society, is the new Messianic Society which is
to be; it is in direct descent from Israel of old. This
Society is the necessary completion of the Messiahship
of Jesus. Towards the realisation or completion of
this Society was St Paul devoting his life.

[1] See Driver's note on the ' Son of Man ' in Dan. vii. 13.
[2] Col. i. 24.

Additional Note on the 'Characteristic Traits' of the 'Servant' in Isaiah, Our Lord, and St Paul.

Professor George Adam Smith notices among the 'Traits' of the Servant mentioned in Isaiah[1], (1) Gentleness[2], (2) Patience[3], (3) Courage[4], (4) Purity[5], (5) Meekness[6], etc.

That these were factors in the character of our Lord needs no proof.

St Paul's insistence upon the need of these virtues in the Christian life, and especially in the ministerial life—the life of service or of 'the servant'—is very striking.

(1) *Gentleness*: διὰ τῆς πραΰτητος καὶ ἐπιεικείας τοῦ χριστοῦ[7], the meekness and gentleness (which are characteristic) of the Christ—both personal and social. St Paul (and other Christians) must thus promote social service.

δοῦλον δὲ κυρίου...δεῖ...ἤπιον εἶναι... ἐν πραΰτητι παιδεύοντα[8],... *i.e.* one who would do service in the servant society.

Also in Titus iii. 2 we have both ἐπιεικεῖς, and πραΰτητα (as virtues needing cultivation).

(2) *Patience*: (ὑπομονή)—as a ministerial trait. ὡς θεοῦ διάκονοι ἐν ὑπομονῇ πολλῇ[9]. | τὰ μὲν σημεῖα τοῦ ἀπο-

---

[1] *Isaiah*, vol. ii. p. 254.
[2] Is. xlii. 2, 3, l. 6, liii. 9 (לֹא־חָמָס עָשָׂה).
[3] Is. xlii. 4, liii. 7.   [4] Is. l. 9.
[5] Is. xli. 15, 16, liii. 9 (וְלֹא מִרְמָה בְּפִיו).
[6] Is. liii. 6, 7, 8.   [7] 2 Cor. x. 1.
[8] 2 Tim. ii. 24.   [9] 2 Cor. vi. 4.

στόλου...ἐν πάσῃ ὑπομονῇ[1]. Add also 1 Tim. vi. 11; 2 Tim. iii. 10, and as a trait of the Christian life Col. i. 11; 2 Thess. i. 4.

(3) *Courage.* Of the Christian Teachers, in Phil. i. 14; of Paul himself, Phil. i. 20; in proclaiming the Gospel, Eph. vi. 19, 20.

(4) *Purity*: (ἁγνότης) as a ministerial trait, 2 Cor. vi. 6, also Phil. i. 16; as a 'Christian' trait, 2 Cor. xi. 3. εἰλικρίνεια in 2 Cor. i. 12, ii. 17.

(5) *Meekness*: (πραΰτης) as a ministerial trait, 1 Cor. iv. 21; 2 Cor. x. 1; 1 Tim. vi. 11; 2 Tim. ii. 25; Tit. iii. 3; and as a Christian virtue, Gal. v. 23; vi. 1; Eph. iv. 2; Col. iii. 21.

In this connection it is interesting to remember that many of these traits are the characteristic virtues of the *socius.*

[1] 2 Cor. xii. 12.

CHAPTER VI.

THE 'CHRIST' OF ST PAUL.

(A.)

St Paul's teaching on this subject is frequently, for more than one reason, difficult to follow. He lived during a period of transition in the use of a term. *Almost* from the first 'Christ' has been to Christians a personal name, or part of a personal name. That it was not so originally we are very apt to forget, and this forgetfulness is made more easy by the constant use of our English versions, where the adjectival use and significance of the word—as a title, or a description, or an office—is almost entirely obscured[1]. This is so in the Authorised Version even in such passages as St Matthew xvi. 16 and St Luke xxiv. 26, where, if the meaning is to be understood, the insertion of the definite article is clearly necessary. In the Revised Version, though the definite article is much more frequently inserted, there are yet passages where its omission is much to be regretted[2].

[1] I am much indebted to an 'additional' note by Bp. Westcott in *Hebrews*, pp. 33 ff. See also Dr Armitage Robinson's *Ephesians*, pp. 22, 32, 42, 43, 44, etc. See also a valuable note by Dr Hort in *First Peter*, pp. 51 ff. See also notes on pp. 25 and 30 ff.

[2] *e.g.* Eph. i. 10, 12, iii. 4, 8, iv. 7, etc.

St Paul himself wrote, as I have just said, in a period of transition in the use of the term. In some cases his use, as that of the Evangelists, is clearly adjectival, in others it is just as clearly personal. There are also not a few instances in which it is hardly possible to come to a decision. [Care must be specially exercised in those cases where Χριστός with the article occurs in the genitive, but preceded by a noun with the article; for in these cases the article may have been inserted for the sake of euphony, *e.g.* 1 Cor. ix. 12, 2 Cor. ii. 12. In each case we might translate either 'the good news of Christ,' or 'the good news of the Messiah.']

In some cases St Paul's insertion, or omission of the article appears to be so pointed, that it seems impossible to doubt that he had a very definite reason for either; and it is evident that in these cases a different connotation must be given to the term as it has, or has not, the definite article. Of this 1 Cor. xv. 22–23 is a striking example: οὕτως καὶ ἐν τῷ χριστῷ πάντες ζωοποιηθήσονται...ἀπαρχὴ Χριστός, ἔπειτα οἱ τοῦ χριστοῦ ἐν τῇ παρουσίᾳ αὐτοῦ. "So also in (or through) the Christ shall all be made alive...Christ the firstfruits, then at His coming those who belong to the Christ." Compare 1 Cor. i. 17, οὐ γὰρ ἀπέστειλέν με Χριστὸς βαπτίζειν...ἵνα μὴ κενωθῇ ὁ σταυρὸς τοῦ χριστοῦ; compare again 1 Cor. i. 12, Ἐγὼ δὲ Χριστοῦ, μεμέρισται ὁ χριστός, μὴ Παῦλος, κ.τ.λ. Where the second clause might be translated, "The Messianic (Society) is torn in pieces."

This last passage suggests a further question. If St Paul's use of ὁ χριστός is sometimes adjectival, then

a substantive, in thought, must be supplied. [We
may compare his use of ἐπουράνιος in the Ephesian
Epistle.] What substantive had he in his mind? When
he speaks of ὁ χριστός (literally the 'Messianic'—)
does he always refer simply to the *personal* Messiah,
to the historic Jesus, now become the *personal* Christ
(or Messiah) of faith? May there be any analogy
with the Old Testament use of 'the Servant'? May
the term be capable of a social as well as of a personal
interpretation, or may the personal also be 'representative'? In other words, may the adjective ὁ χριστός
sometimes refer to the Messianic Society, of which the
Personal Messiah is at once the Head and the Representative, in whom all the members are represented[1]?
As instances which might bear this interpretation I
would cite the following:—1 Cor. xii. 12, τὸ σῶμα ἕν
ἐστιν καὶ μέλη πολλὰ ἔχει, πάντα δὲ τὰ μέλη τοῦ σώματος
πολλὰ ὄντα ἕν ἐστιν σῶμα, οὕτως καὶ ὁ χριστός (the Messianic Society). Cp. *v.* 14, καὶ γὰρ τὸ σῶμα οὐκ ἔστιν ἓν
μέλος ἀλλὰ πολλά; or Rom. ix. 3, ηὐχόμην γὰρ ἀνάθεμα
εἶναι αὐτὸς ἐγὼ ἀπὸ τοῦ χριστοῦ ὑπὲρ τῶν ἀδελφῶν, "I
could wish, even I, that I were anathema from the
Messianic (Society) for the sake of my brethren,"
[Anathema here means, practically,'excommunicated'],
or Rom. xv. 3, καὶ γὰρ ὁ χριστὸς οὐχ ἑαυτῷ ἤρεσεν. For in
the Old Testament portrayal of Him the Messianic
(One, or Society) pleased not Himself[2] (it was not

---

[1] By this Society or Body is, of course, to be understood the
society or social-body now in communion with the living personal
Messiah, *i.e.* the exalted personal Christ.

[2] See a note in Bp. Westcott's *Hebrews*, on The Body of Christ,
pp. 340 ff.

'characteristic' of Him to do so); also Rom. vii. 4,
διὰ τοῦ σώματος τοῦ χριστοῦ, "Wherefore my brethren
ye also were made dead to the law through (your
incorporation into) the body of the Christ." For the
death of Christ (personal) was the condition of the
existence of the Christ- (the Spirit-) inspired Society.

(B.)

It is in the Epistle to the Ephesians that St Paul's
teaching of the Universal Messianic Society is most
clearly expressed, and there it is found in connection
with another idea, which gives a very helpful key both
to its meaning and its application. I mean the idea,
to which I have already alluded, of the personal Christ
receiving in the life of the Christian (or Messianic)
Society His 'fulfilment.'

In order to understand this Epistle we must notice
carefully its continuity of thought with the Old
Testament[1]. In a very true sense St Paul does not
regard the Christian Society, the Church, as a new
Society : it is rather the direct, and true, and legitimate continuation and development of the old Divine
Society, the covenant people of Israel[2]. The Epistle
when carefully read is found to be full of references

[1] "Under His" (the Holy Spirit's) "action the Church becomes in
its turn the complete representative of the Messiah upon earth."
(W. Lock, *St Paul, the Master Builder*, p. 46.)

[2] τοῖς ἁγίοις (i. 1) : see Lightfoot on *Philipp*. i. 1. "The Christian
Church having taken the place of the Jewish race has inherited all its
titles and privileges."

to, and of ideas drawn from, the Old Testament. Take
the great passage with which it opens : this is simply
crowded with Old Testament references, and we may
assert that it cannot be understood or appreciated
apart from a careful recollection of the significance of
these references : *e.g.*

ἐν πάσῃ εὐλογίᾳ πνευματικῇ : in opposition to the
material blessings under the old covenant.

ἐξελέξατο ἡμᾶς : as He 'chose' Israel of old; we are
His 'chosen' people. A very common idea in the
Prophets. The Chosen One, a well-known title of
Messiah. Is. xlii. 1. (Quoted, and applied to our Lord
in St Matt. xii. 18.)

εἰς υἱοθεσίαν : the true position of the Messianic
people.

ἐν τῷ ἠγαπημένῳ : a Messianic title.

These are only examples, and they might easily be
increased in number.

But it is when we come to the tenth verse, where
the object is stated, that we begin to see the full
significance of the passage. ἀνακεφαλαιώσασθαι τὰ πάντα
ἐν τῷ χριστῷ : "to gather up in one all things (the
Universe) in the Messiah." Here "the stress is not
laid on the individual personality, but rather on the
Messianic office[1]. The Messiah summed up the Ancient
People : St Paul proclaims that He sums up the
Universe[2]." Is not God's 'secret' to be unfolded and

---

[1] Armitage Robinson *in loc.* (p. 32).

[2] "The man who has most worked himself into the heart of the
apostolic thought will most wonder, if we may so speak, at its daring
completeness, at the splendid courage with which it embraces God
and man, time and eternity in one immense and harmonious system.
And this system is, as it were, epitomized in Christ; it all stood

God's purpose achieved in the new realisation of the Messianic idea which is to be expressed in and through the Messianic Society?

It is easier to pursue this line of thought in verses 11 and 12 in Greek than in English; for ἐν αὐτῷ, ἐν ᾧ, and ἐν τῷ χριστῷ, may in the Greek refer either to 'Christ' (personal) or to Messiah (official)—as an *idea*, or doctrine, or purpose (including in 'Messiah' a possible *social* connotation); and then we might interpret thus:— "in the working out of this purpose, realised already in, and taking its new development from (the personal) Christ, we have received our 'portion[1]'...we who were the first to hope in the Messiah."

I next turn to *vv.* 19 ff.: " According to the working of the might of His strength, which He hath wrought in the Messiah, having raised Him from the dead...and gave Him (as) head over all things to the Church, which is His body, the fulness of Him Who all in all is being fulfilled." To understand these verses we must consider the whole passage in which they occur, *i.e. vv.* 15–23.

The starting-point is faith in Jesus as Lord[2] (ἐν τῷ

together in Him, a universe whose unity was its head " (A. M. Fairbairn, *The City of God*, p. 250).

[1] ἐκληρώθημεν : Armitage Robinson quotes Deut. xxxii. 8 ff. and Zech. ii. 12.

[2] On the use of Κύριος as a Messianic Title in the *Psalms of Solomon*, see art. under that title in *Hastings' Bib. Dict.*

There is an illuminating chapter in Dr A. M. Fairbairn's *The City of God* (pp. 245 ff.) on " The Jesus of History and the Christ of Faith ": see especially the passage (p. 249), " If the speech of our modern schools were here allowed us, we might say that the name ' Christ ' represented to the Apostles a philosophy of God, of Nature, and of Man " (I would venture to add to these words, " and also of Society "). Dr Fairbairn himself seems to suggest this on p. 250.

κυρίῳ Ἰησοῦ); then St Paul looks to the God of our
Lord (Jesus)—Messiah; this God shall cause them to
know 'the past, the future, and, not least, the present';
(1) the *past* speaks of " the hope of His calling," (2) the
future of " the riches of the glory of His inheritance in
the saints " (N.B. the Old Testament terms ' glory,'
' inheritance,' ' saints' have a future meaning. "The
Lord's portion is His people: Jacob is the lot of His
inheritance[1]"), (3) the *present* speaks of "the exceeding
greatness of His power to usward who believe." This
power has been recently manifested in His raising the
Messiah (personal) from the dead...and in subduing
all things under His feet—as the representative of the
human race—and in appointing Him as head over all
things to the Church—the ideal human (Messianic)
Society, which is the necessary fulness, or fulfilment,
of Him (the Messiah) Who is all in all in process of
being fulfilled.

To gain a clear conception of this passage several
points must be simultaneously kept in view :—

I. (1) The hope of God's calling is God's purpose[2]
(as yet unfulfilled), a Messianic Society co-extensive
with the human race.

(2) The wealth of God's glory. The wealth which
manifests God's glory, and *Gloria Dei vivens homo*,

[1] Deut. xxxii. 9.

[2] With this cp. the passage iii. 1 ff. especially νοῆσαι τὴν σύνεσίν
μου ἐν τῷ μυστηρίῳ τοῦ χριστοῦ. " The, as yet, not unfolded (yet in the
process of being unfolded) secret, or rather 'partially hidden plan '
of the Messianic—(society?). The plan of a universal society in
which Jew and Gentile should live on equal terms."

hence the 'glory' is the innumerable multitudes of the ἅγιοι in the ages to come.

(3) God's tremendous power towards all believers has been proved in the raising of the Christ. We must note the term ἐν τῷ χριστῷ, 'in the *sphere* of the Messiah[1].' This is the sphere in which the divine δύναμις has been, and is to be, especially energetic.

II. When the thought is concentrated upon the *personal*, and already victorious and ruling Messiah, it is at once seen to be incomplete. Another exercise of the divine δύναμις is seen in the ἔδωκεν ('appointed' in the divine counsels as supreme head to the Church). [We must also bear in mind the passage in 1 Cor. xii. 12 ff. In Ephesians, as Dr Armitage Robinson states, we have a picture, as it were, of the Christ with His head in heaven, but His body still upon earth. In the passages in 1st Corinthians the Christ is *identified* with the members, and the thought of the Head *and* the members does not enter. It is in the unity and diversity of the members that the one body is constituted. The Messianic body (ὁ χριστός) is here on earth; all believers are individually and collectively ἐν Χριστῷ. At the same time, as in Ephesians, when the Head is regarded as by the side of the body (its πλήρωμα)—the Head there and the body here—there is no want of unity.]

III. Yet another line of thought should simultaneously be kept in view, viz. that suggested by the quotation from Ps. viii. which contains the question, "What is man?" and in which it is asserted that under the feet of man all things have been put.

[1] Cf. ἐν τῷ πονηρῷ, 1 Joh. v. 19.

By the writer of the Epistle to the Hebrews this Psalm
is regarded and expounded as 'Messianic.' But as
yet, that is as far as man generally is concerned,
this 'putting under' is clearly unfulfilled, though it
is fulfilled in 'Jesus.' In 1 Cor. xv. 20 ff. we have
a passage which should also be read in connection
with this. In *v.* 23 we have both the connection and
the distinction between χριστός and οἱ τοῦ χριστοῦ, and
here again the thought of future subjection is as
yet unrealised. Again we may refer to St Stephen's
vision, where we have the term 'Son of Man,' so
rare in the New Testament except in the mouth of
our Lord Himself, and for which therefore we may
assume there was some special reason. We must
notice that the term stands side by side with the
'glory of God,' with 'Jesus,' with the 'heavens
opened,' and with 'standing at the right hand of God.'

Careful meditation upon this speech, which St
Paul must have heard, suggests these ideas in close
connection with each other :—'Heaven,' the vision
and home of the ideal yet to be realised; the 'glory
of God,' the vision of the purpose which 'glorifies'
God, revealed in Jesus, the representative man, who is
'standing,' and therefore in the act of bringing about
the fulfilment of some purpose; at 'the right hand,'
and therefore in a position of authority and power.

That to the Jews there was something very
definite, and very dangerous, and 'far-reaching in
suggestion,' implied in these words we must conclude
from the intensity of their rage which issued in the
immediate violent death of Stephen[1].

[1] Sabatier, *L'Apôtre Paul*, p. 26.

(C.)

I have considered these passages at some length because I believe that in them and similar passages we shall find the true key to St Paul's Social Teaching. Every great social teacher (and such was St Paul) will have some *ideal* of Society. He will have a clear conception not only of what it is, but of what it is meant to be and to do[1]. And we must notice that St Paul does not only put before us an ideal of society, he clearly states his conception of the ideal *Socius*[2]— the perfect man, socially regarded—the ideal unit of society. And it is by indefinite multiplication of examples of this ideal *socius*, in each of which his qualities are reproduced, that the ideal society grows[3].

When St Paul accepted Jesus as the Messiah he accepted Him as the perfect realisation of the Divine will, so far as the Divine conception of man is concerned. But a perfect individual with perfect social qualities can only be an earnest, a promise, a 'prophecy' (in the true sense of the word). For perfect social faculties presuppose the possibility of a perfect society, in which these qualities can find a field for their exercise; thus the perfect man can only be the "firstborn among many brethren." St Paul saw that the Old Testament, in which is contained the revelation of God's will in the past, was full of *social* hopes, of the hope of a perfect society. But until Jesus came, and until He proved Himself victorious

---

[1] See Additional Note on 'The Realism of St Paul,' p. 142.
[2] See p. 93.   [3] See p. 88.

over death (and sin) and thus received the mark of the
Divine approbation, the perfect individual, the germ,
the perfect seed (the perfect *socius*), from whom the
perfect society should spring, or be developed, had
never come. Now, in Him, the *possibility* was at length
realised, and in the indefinite multiplication of like-
nesses (in Spirit[1]) to Him should the perfect society
consist[2]. But Jesus, according to the flesh, sprang from
God's chosen people. And God had in the past worked
along definite lines, chosen according to His own wisdom. He had revealed Himself,—His character, His
virtues, His will, His purpose,—to a definite people, a
prophetic people, whose representative men the prophets were[3]. The greatest of these portrayed the people
of God as a *servant* chosen and ordained to do God's
will, but this prophecy, if once clearly expressed in the
experiences of an individual[4], had never been fulfilled,
until Jesus, so far as an individual could fulfil it, had
done this. But, being the expression of a social purpose,

---

[1] The following line of thought seems to deserve at least consideration : Because I believe in the Holy Spirit, *therefore* I believe
in the Holy Catholic Church—the perfect, world-wide, mankind-
embracing society. But 'the Holy Spirit' is 'the Spirit of Christ.'
Note especially 2 Cor. iii. 12–18. (1) The failure of the O.T. society.
(2) In turning to the Lord lies the hope of success. (3) The Lord
is the Spirit who 'enables' us towards, and guarantees, the true
development; and this is wrought through reflection of His 'glory'—
His essential perfection. Thus we (socially), as the N.T. society, are
continuously and progressively transformed towards the ideal.

[2] Yet not so as to destroy the 'organic' nature of the society,
see *infra*.

[3] Davidson, *O.T. Prophecy*, p. 5.

[4] Is. liii. (?).

it must have not only an individual, but a social, fulfilment. All the history, all the revelation of the past,
pointed to this. Hence only in a society of those made
like to the perfect individual (to Jesus), that is only in
His disciples, could the purpose of God, the ideal society,
be realised and fulfilled.

I spoke just now of the ideal society consisting of
the indefinite multiplication of individuals like to Jesus.
But St Paul never regards society as a mere aggregate
of individuals. To him even the universal society, which
is to embrace mankind, is always an 'organic unity[1].'
To him the Messianic Society does not grow simply by
addition of members like each other. As in other
organisms, the growth of society proceeds both by
multiplication of individuals and by differentiation of
function. In his favourite similes of the human body
and its members, and of the building and its separate
parts, St Paul sets before us most clearly the idea of
unity with diversity. The very idea of society as an
'organism' assumes that the members have various
functions, and this thought is made still more clear
when we remember his teaching about the dependence
of the members, not only upon the Head, but upon
each other. And there is variety not only among the
members, but there is variety in the *relationships*
between the members[2]; and to St Paul the healthy
condition of these relationships is essential to the
health of the body and of all the members. In all this
teaching St Paul is absolutely in agreement with ex-

[1] N.B. Eph. iv.; 1 Cor. xii.
[2] Col. ii. 19.

perience, and his cosmopolitan education and breadth of sympathy enabled him to appreciate the service rendered to humanity by men of different nations (indeed by different nations themselves) with different ideas[1]. His knowledge of the Imperial System, its unity, its variety of function and service, its network of lines of communication, physical and political, by means of which relations between the centre and the provinces, and between the provinces with each other, were regularly maintained, must have been a constant example of his own teaching. Here there was one supreme head, and one power conveyed through a multitude of different channels, and finding expression in many smaller societies and institutions, as well as in the activity of thousands of officials, all ultimately responsible to, and representing, the Head. And the force which maintained and kept in motion this vast system was 'the Empire.' In a very true sense 'the idea' was its life. Here we may see an example of St Paul's teaching that the spiritual, in one sense the ideal, is not only the real, but the *only* real.

[1] Cp. Rev. xxi. 26.

CHAPTER VII.

ST PAUL'S TEACHING AND MODERN SOCIOLOGY.

(INTRODUCTORY NOTE.)

IT must be remembered that Sociology as a scientific study is of recent growth, and that it has until within the last few years found comparatively few students in England. But since the establishment of the Sociological Society in London, two years ago, the study has received a strong impetus; and considering the practical benefits which may accrue from a more careful investigation into, not only the facts (the 'Statics'), but the relations and processes (the 'Kinetics' and 'Kinematics'), of society, the study will in the future in all probability claim many more workers. Sociology at present labours under many obvious disadvantages, not the least of which is that even the name itself is still used by different writers with somewhat different meanings, *e.g.* occasionally it is used as if synonymous with 'Social Philosophy' (which should rather refer to the teleology—the conscious aims—of Society); occasionally, again, it is still employed as a kind of generic term to cover a number of more or less closely related fields of investigation including anthropology, archaeology, some aspects of history, social economics, and the problems of poverty—all these being pursued rather as related fields of knowledge than as parts of the same field. But it is, I think, now being gradually recognised that in its true sense Sociology is the study of *all* social facts, relations, and processes, to which all these studies (including of course social psychology) are contributory.

Improved and enlarged materials for the study are rapidly accumulating even in this country, *e.g.* the recently published volumes of *Sociological Papers*, issued by the Sociological Society. The importance of the study to those engaged in any branch of social work will not be denied[1].

A comparison of St Paul's social teaching, or that of our Lord, with the teaching gained from an investigation, inductively pursued, into social facts and processes may also serve a useful 'apologetic' purpose[2]. Recently Christian apologetics have exhibited a tendency to dwell relatively less upon the authenticity of witness to historical events which took place in the past, and more, first upon the power of Christianity to satisfy the deepest needs of man, and secondly upon the correctness of the New Testament 'philosophy of man' when tested by personal experience. So

[1] See a very interesting article in *Hibbert Journal* for Oct. 1905, by Prof. Henry Jones, *The Working Faith of the Social Reformer.* "No one who is interested in the social well-being of the people will deny that amongst the deepest needs of our times is the need of clear light upon the broad principles of social well-being;—the need, in short, of *a science of social life.*"

[2] On this subject see further, p. 144.

I believe the social teaching of the New Testament
when read in the light of the most scientifically pursued
research into the problems of society will prove to be
at least equally true to experience, and equally capable
of solving the problems of society.

In the comparisons in the chapter which follows
I have chosen as an example of modern sociological
teaching a work which follows strictly the inductive
method, because I believe from experience in other
fields of scientific research this is the method which
may be expected to yield the most trustworthy results.
Of course as the field for investigation is so vast, and
the work as yet done in it is so small, the results so
far obtained can only be regarded as very tentative.
Still, as the following pages will show, some of these
results reveal a striking coincidence with many of the
articles of St Paul's social creed.

(A.)

The more carefully we study St Paul's social
teaching the more clearly will two closely related
truths force themselves upon our attention:—

The *first* is that to him the Christian (the Messianic),
that is the ideal, society is only natural human society
'at its best,' that is 'raised to the highest point of
possibility'; it is society as it should be, and as it was
meant to be[1].

[1] I have shown elsewhere that St Paul conceives the society he
describes in Eph. iv. as already existing. See also reference to
Hort's *Christian Ecclesia*, on p. 2.

The *second* is that St Paul has anticipated very many of the truths, or laws, or conclusions arrived at by the most careful and thorough investigations into the 'science' of society; or, to express this somewhat differently, that investigations into this science inductively conducted, entirely prove the correctness of St Paul's social teaching. Thus we may say that between St Paul's social teaching and the principles of modern sociology, regarded as an exact science, there is a very striking agreement. As an example of a recent scientific exposition of the Science of Society I would take Professor Giddings' *Inductive Sociology*, and I will now try to show how St Paul's teaching is in very close agreement with his conclusions.

[It will be understood that in an investigation covering so wide a field I must limit myself to giving a comparatively few illustrations of this agreement.]

To the sociologist the unit of investigation is the *socius*, that is, 'the individual in his *social* capacity'— man as a companion, a learner, teacher, co-worker, etc.

[It is, of course, necessary to point out that our conception of the *socius* presupposes our psychological[1] conception of him. Hence a complete study of St Paul's social teaching should include a study of St Paul's psychology of man. For this study, except very indirectly, I have no space. But it is worth notice how very great stress St Paul again and again lays upon one forming a correct impression of man's

---

[1] Many hints towards a study of St Paul's psychology may be found in the Art. 'Psychology' in *Hastings*' *B. D.* iv. pp. 163 ff. See also the Bibliography appended to that article.

nature, and of the possibilities of the transformation of that nature under the influence of Christianity.]

For the perfection of society it will be seen that we must have the perfection of the *socius*, that is, of man in his social capacity. We must seek therefore for means to develop man's social qualities and activities.

It is an instructive study to notice the qualities of the *socius* as manifested in our Lord's character (as this is portrayed by the Evangelists). I refer, of course, to the virtues He displayed in His dealings with others. It will be found that the social virtues upon the cultivation of which St Paul laid special stress are the same as those we find so active in our Lord[1].

The following may be regarded as the chief activities of the *socius*. [A little reflection will show how active St Paul himself was in these, and how eagerly he encouraged others in their discharge.]

(1) *Loving and seeking acquaintance, and forming friendship and alliances with other* socii *like himself*[2].

Inasmuch as St Paul was a *Missionary*[3] he was always seeking acquaintance with others. His capacity for forming friendships is an outstanding trait of his character; we have only to think of Barnabas, Silas, Luke, Timothy, Aquila and Priscilla, and to recall the many names in Rom. xvi. and Col. iv. He did not

[1] Sanday and Headlam, *Romans*, p. 381.

[2] Giddings, p. 10.

[3] Man in his 'missionary' capacity—in the fullest sense of the word—may be regarded as a high development of the *socius*.

bear loneliness or solitude well. Bishop Lightfoot[1] has pointed out how in one of the saddest periods of his life, St Paul's low spirits seem to have been intensified by his temporary want of companionship.

(2) *Imitating others, teaching them and learning from them*[2]. St Paul, with his wide knowledge of human nature and of social forces, lays great stress upon the power of *imitation*. His own object is to imitate Christ (personal); he calls upon those whom he is teaching to imitate him (1 Cor. xi. 1; 1 Thess. i. 6; 1 Cor. iv. 16). He dwells also upon the power of *example* (1 Tim. iv. 12). The width of his knowledge and his eclecticism shows how constant a *learner* he must have been. He gave his life to teaching.

(3) *Engaging with others in many forms of common activity*[2]. The record of St Paul's life from the time of his conversion is one continuous record of co-operation with others. He rarely, and never from choice, works alone. The practical lesson which he draws from the contemplation of society as an organism is the opportunity and need of the co-operation of the various members, each engaged in the fulfilment of his particular function, but 'working together'—united in, and by, one spirit, and endeavouring to effect one common purpose, *e.g.* 1 Cor. xii. 4 ff.

In this connection I would draw attention to St Paul's insistence upon the cultivation and maintenance of those ethical qualities which make possible co-operation, friendship, etc. He lays stress upon the need of unity of spirit (Eph. iv. 3); of unity of mind

---

[1] *Galatians*, p. 39.   [2] Giddings, p. 10.

(Phil. i. 27, ii. 2); he is insistent upon the cultivation of the peaceful temper (Rom. xiv. 19; 1 Cor. vii. 15; 2 Cor. xiii. 11), and upon entering into the position and views of others (1 Cor. ix. 20), and upon humility (Eph. iv. 2), etc.

Another truth we learn from modern scientific sociology is that *conduct depends upon response to external* stimuli[1]. These *stimuli* are of various kinds, they may be something we see or hear, also new ideas gathered from reading a book, or from hearing a speech. All these stimuli produce sensations which are of the nature of changes in our state of consciousness. Upon these certain reactions, that is activities of mind or body, take place. The sum of these activities is the total response to stimulation, and they assume certain definite and practical modes, and they concentrate themselves upon certain practical achievements. These modes of activity may be said to be four, and they have been named :—(1) *Appreciation,* or the sum of the mental processes—knowledge, preference, valuation—constituting an attitude of mind towards our environment; (2) *Utilization,* or the deliberate and systematic adaptation of the external world to ourselves; (3) *Characterization,* or the adaptation of ourselves to the external world; and (4) *Socialization,* which is the attempt to adapt ourselves to one another. [Success in this last 'mode of activity' will be dependent upon success in the three previous modes.]

St Paul's ideals, whether social or individual, for his converts are often found in his prayers on their

[1] Giddings, p. 57.

behalf. In his prayer for the Philippian Church
(i. 9 ff.) he prays that these four modes of activity may
be realised in the lives of its members. (1) "This,
I pray, that your love"—a synonym for 'Christianity'
which lays stress on its social activity, as well as upon
its divine inspiration—"may abound yet more and more
in knowledge and every kind of discernment" (ἐν ἐπι-
γνώσει καὶ πάσῃ αἰσθήσει)—the means of *appreciation*
(perception, cognition, and discrimination); (2) "so
that ye may approve" (εἰς τὸ δοκιμάζειν) "the things that
excel"; here we have the practical testing with a view
to permanent *utilization*; (3) "that ye may be sincere
and void of offence unto the day of Christ": this is
characterization as the result upon themselves of the
use of the things which have been chosen; (4) "being
filled with the fruit of righteousness" (δικαιοσύνης).
This is *socialization*, for δικαιοσύνη must at least include
the right discharge of all social relationships.

Another, if somewhat less obvious example is
found in St Paul's prayer for the Colossian Church
(i. 9 ff.) :—(1) "Filled with the knowledge of His will"
(*appreciation*); (2) "walk worthily" (wise *utilization*
of circumstances); (3) "all patience and long suffering"
(*characterization*); (4) "meet to be partakers of the
inheritance" (*socialization*). Yet another example may
be traced in Ephesians, Chapter ii.

Thus we may assert that St Paul is practically in
entire agreement with the latest scientific theory or
explanation as to the modes of development of the
'social personality'—as to the manner in which the
socius is evolved. The practical aim and work of the
Christian teacher must, of course, be the creation and

exhibition of the highest stimuli and the effort to bring these stimuli to act upon as many people as possible, cf. Col. i. 28 ὅν ἡμεῖς καταγγέλλομεν (proclaim) νουθετοῦντες πάντα ἄνθρωπον, κ.τ.λ., Gal. iii. 1 οἷς κατ' ὀφθαλμοὺς Ἰησοῦς Χριστὸς προεγράφη (was placarded) ἐσταυρωμένος, 1 Cor. i. 23, etc. This must be done in order that the processes of 'perception,' 'cognition,' and 'appreciation' may be widely made active, and that men may, through clear perception and adequate knowledge, appreciate Him,—His character, His virtues, His work, His sacrifice; that they may utilise life and the world after His example, and then, having become characterized by His Spirit and after His likeness, they may behave to others as He did. Thus the Christian social-man and the Christian society are developed and extended.

Modern Sociology speaks of 'The Moral Sense of the Community[1],' of 'Public Opinion,' of 'the Public Will'; and we know what powerful agents each of these may be. The statesman and the reformer (and the Christian is bound to be a reformer) seek to influence both public opinion and the public will, for the opinion governs the will. Through the public will are practical reforms accomplished.

One aspect of St Paul's work may be regarded as the effort to create a certain 'social mind' which may become a social *force*[2]. This social mind is created by arousing like response to the same stimuli applied to many minds: this is followed by 'awareness of similar response,' and by 'consciousness

[1] Giddings, p. 65.
[2] Ramsay, *Seven Churches*, p. 135.

of kind.' From this comes the possibility of 'concerted volition' which acts with controlling power upon individuals.

St Paul lays the greatest stress upon the creation, the fostering, and the strengthening of this social mind, which is a social force, and also upon the responsibility of the exercise of this force. Philipp. i. 27 ὅτι στήκετε ἐν ἑνὶ πνεύματι, μιᾷ ψυχῇ συναθλοῦντες…, cp. ii. 2 ἵνα τὸ αὐτὸ φρονῆτε τὴν αὐτὴν ἀγάπην ἔχοντες, σύνψυχοι, τὸ ἓν φρονοῦντες. He calls for the exercise of a social force at Corinth (1 Cor. v. 4); again in 2 Thess. iii. 11 (in the case of the idle and disorderly, who by such conduct are guilty of social sins). Here St Paul appeals to the moral sense of the community (which their profession of Christianity presupposes),—to the social mind which is to set in motion a social force,—to withhold from the man so acting the advantages of the life of the community.

Modern Scientific Sociology teaches us that societies are of two kinds—'component' and 'constituent[1].' A component society is 'wholly or partly a genetic aggregation.' Its members share as much mental or moral resemblance as may be necessary for practical cooperation: among the members are found, and tolerated, differences of ability, of character, and of taste. So long as the aggregate of resemblances remains large and varied, the mental and moral differences of a component society may be of any imaginable kind. A family, a village, a town, a kingdom, 'the Roman Empire,' are all examples of a 'component' society.

[1] Giddings, p. 187.

Now a constituent society is an "association for carrying on a particular activity, for achieving some special social end[1]," having "a defined object in view; it is purposive in character." "Its members are supposed to be aware of its object, and to put forth effort for its attainment."…"New members are admitted into a purposive association only by their own consent, and by the permission of members."…"Purposive associations have no independent existence…they presuppose the social constitution."

"The component society…may tolerate much diversity of mental and moral traits;…in matters of detail it is willing to tolerate difference. In the constituent society it is precisely a matter of detail that is of chief concern. In constituent societies therefore likeness of nationality…may to a great extent be ignored, but actual agreement of mind and character upon the specific object for which the association exists is required[2]."

A very little reflexion will show how St Paul realised and expressed all these truths. The following references will suffice :—(1) The Church as a purposive association: to "present every man perfect in Christ," Col. i. 28. (2) This end is *social*, "till we all attain unto the unity of the faith…according to the working in due measure of each several part…," Eph. iv. 13, 16.   (3) St Paul frequently appeals to the knowledge which his converts possess of the purpose, Eph. iii. 9, 18; compare his stress upon prophecy and upon the office of the understanding 1 Cor. xiv.   (4) From the earliest times it has been of the essence of baptism—the ceremony of entrance—

[1] Giddings, p. 199.   [2] *Ibid.* p. 200.

that it should be voluntary, and public, *i.e.* that the entrance of a new member into the Church should be sanctioned by the other members.   (5) In a very true sense the Church has 'no independent existence' and 'it has always presupposed the social constitution,' hence St Paul's stress upon obedience to the civil, or imperial authority, and his exhortation for intercession on behalf of that authority.   (6) 'Matters of detail,' *e.g.* carefulness of faith and conduct, are of vital importance in the Christian life, 1 Cor. x. 14 ff. and xi., Gal. vi., and St Paul's exhortations generally. (7) Likeness of nationality is ignored. "There cannot be Greek and Jew...barbarian, Scythian," Col. iii. 11. (8) Actual agreement of mind and character is demanded. "Perfected together in the same mind and the same judgment," 1 Cor. i. 10.   "That ye be of the same mind, having the same love, being of one accord," Phil. ii. 2; and especially is agreement demanded upon the specific object of the association, *i.e.* making men like Christ, Phil. ii. 5, "Have this mind in you which was also in Christ Jesu," "that ye may grow up in all things into Him which is the Head even Christ," Eph. iv. 15.

Inductive Sociology shows that within a large purposive association, or 'constituent society,' there may be smaller purposive associations, each of which associations has a social function.   Also we see among these evidence of purposive grouping or functional association.

As the original association develops these grow; yet not by mere increase of mass, or aggregation of units, but by differentiation of function.

In Acts xx. 17 the elders of the Church in Ephesus

are not regarded simply as a body of individuals but as a body within the society. In Eph. iv. 11 the apostles, prophets, evangelists, pastors, and teachers, may be similarly regarded. And in the pastoral epistles, where we find a further development of the society, and, in consequence, a further differentiation of function, this truth is still more evident.

For 'efficiency of organisation' in any society Professor Giddings[1] shows that at least the following conditions are necessary.

(1) The loyal and earnest co-operation of its members, and their devotion to the society.

In Rom. xii. 6 we are shown how every 'gift' and opportunity must be fully employed for the common benefit—ministry, teaching, liberal giving, diligent ruling; in *v.* 10 "Love of the brethren" is enjoined; in *v.* 13 the communicating to the necessity of the saints; in Rom. xvi. we are told how Aquila and Priscilla "laid down their necks" for St Paul, and if for him, then for the society he was extending. In 1 Cor. xvi. we have the collection for the saints, and the house of Stephanas ministering to the saints; in 2 Cor. xi. the brethren from Macedonia are commended for supplying St Paul's wants, etc., etc.

(2) The members must be convinced that they actually share and secure the benefits of the association. On the other hand those who compose the governing circles must not forget that they are the servants of the entire association.

We have only to think again of the speech to the

[1] p. 228 ff.

Ephesian elders to see how insistent St Paul is upon
the realisation of these conditions: the whole flock
(παντὶ τῷ ποιμνίῳ) is to be shepherded and fed; false
teachers, as happened in Galatia (Gal. vi. 12, 13), will
think of themselves, not of all the members of the body:
the weak are to be helped, Acts xx. 35; and giving
is more blessed than receiving. In Col. ii. 18 no man
is to be robbed of his prize; in Col. i. 28 every man
is to be presented perfect in Christ, for this St Paul
labours. In Acts xx. 33, 34, St Paul shows that he has
made no personal profit. He regards his own office as
a stewardship, or a ministry. It is not his office, but
his ministry which is to be glorified (τὴν διακονίαν μου
δοξάζω)[1]. In all this he is only showing himself to be
filled and inspired by the spirit of Jesus.

(3) "The efficiency of social organization depends
upon a recognition of the vital importance of expert
knowledge. Fitness, shown by the successful performance of duty in subordinate positions, shall be
the sole ground of advancement to positions of greater
responsibility[2]." [All this largely depends upon recog-
nising the advantage of a division of labour in the
development of the society.]

Compare St Paul's insistence upon qualification,
in previous life and performance of duty, for office,
1 Tim. iii. 1, 5, 6, 7, 13. Timothy must be an example
(1 Tim. iv. 12), he must proceed in self-education
(iv. 13); the widows must have gained a good re-
putation through good works (v. 10); the elders who
rule well must be counted worthy of double honour;
especially those who have made themselves experts in
knowledge and capacity to teach (v. 16), etc., etc.

[1] Rom. xi. 13.   [2] Giddings, p. 231.

(B.)

Another great truth upon which modern Scientific Sociology insists is that a final test of the efficiency of a social organisation lies especially in its power to develop "an improving type of human personality[1]." The following assertions will hardly be controverted. "The social welfare is the sum of the ends for which Society exists"; "To secure and to perfect the social welfare is the social function"; "The ends for which Society exists are: (1) *Proximate*—certain general conditions of well being, external to the individual personality, but necessary for its perfection and happiness, (2) *Ultimate*—'The Social Personality.' For '*life* itself is the ultimate social end,' but 'not life irrespective of form or quality.' 'It is life in its higher developments which society exists to perfect,' *i.e.* to create a social personality 'adapted to social co-operation and enjoyment.' Thus the Social Personality, 'the moral, intellectual, social man, the highest product of evolution, is the ultimate end of social organisation[2].'"

This is almost, if not entirely, in accordance with St Paul's own teaching. In Eph. iv. 1 ff. St Paul (incidentally) describes both the faith and the organisation of the Christian Society. The ultimate end of the organisation is πρὸς τὸν καταρτισμὸν τῶν ἁγίων εἰς ἔργον διακονίας[3], for the perfecting, or equipment, of the saints

---

[1] Giddings, p. 232.   [2] *Ibid.* p. 233.
[3] No comma before εἰς.

with a view to (mutual) ministerial work; each
member must be made perfect in order that he may
render perfect social service; this will imply the
perfection of each individual. Again in *v.* 13, "till
we all come to the unity of the faith and of the [full][1]
knowledge of the Son of God, unto a perfect man," etc.
Unity can only be reached when both faith and knowledge are perfect, for it implies in both identity with
the truth—the ideal. It is quite true that εἰς ἄνδρα
τέλειον cannot mean 'perfect men,' which might mean
that the perfect society was simply an aggregation of
perfect individuals, all exactly alike; which would
destroy the social idea. It implies rather each coming
to the absolute possible fulness of his *own* moral,
spiritual, intellectual, and social growth. (*Vide* the next
clause ἵνα μηκέτι ὦμεν νήπιοι, and therefore with the
possibilities [and duty] of growth yet unfulfilled.)
With this passage we may compare 1 Thess. v. 11 διὸ
παρακαλεῖτε ἀλλήλους καὶ οἰκοδομεῖτε εἰς τὸν ἕνα; the social
act of each member of the society endeavouring to
help each individual in the development towards perfection. Again Rom. xiii. 8, He that loveth (and
therefore is prepared to make practical self-sacrifice
for) his neighbour (for his improvement) hath fulfilled
the [divine] law. Rom. xiv. 19; we are to follow
things whereby we may edify one another. 1 Cor. iii.
23; for all things are yours, *e.g.* the services of the
Christian teachers, and the activities of the Society.
1 Cor. x. 23; the difference between unsocial (un-

---

[1] I am not convinced by Dr Armitage Robinson [*Ephesians*,
p. 248 ff.] *contra* Lightfoot, etc. as to the meaning of ἐπίγνωσις.

edifying) and social (edifying) conduct: compare also
the whole argument about spiritual gifts, love, prophecy,
and tongues, in 1 Cor. xii.-xiv. Tongues are of little
value, because they are unsocial, and they do not
edify. Prophecy, and above all love, does edify. Note
especially chap. xiv. 3, 6, 12, 17.

We must now notice how careful St Paul is with
regard to the establishment and maintenance of what
Prof. Giddings calls 'Proximate Ends' or 'Public
Utilities[1].' These are necessary for the development
of the perfect 'social personality'; because they are
necessary for that condition of society—that environment—which conduces to this development. These
'Proximate Ends' may be grouped under four heads:
—(1) " *Security*, of life and possessions, maintained by
the political system; (2) *Liberty and Justice*, maintained by the legal system; (3) *material well-being*
created by the economic system; (4) the knowledge of
and command over nature, created by the cultural
system."

(1) St Paul insists strongly upon the maintenance
of the civil or political order. Rom. xiii. 1-7. "Sup-
plications, prayers, intercessions, thanksgivings are to
be made...for kings and all that are in high place.
That we may live a quiet and tranquil life[2]." St Paul
constantly insists upon the cultivation of the peaceful
temper as creating a peaceful atmosphere in which the
individual and the society may develop[3].

---

[1] p. 232.   [2] 1 Tim. ii. 1 ff.
[3] Rom. xiv. 19; 2 Cor. xiii. 11 ; 1 Thess. v. 13 ; etc.

(2)   The enjoyment of liberty and justice might be regarded as among the benefits of civil order.   But St Paul insists also upon justice between members of the Church; to wrong, oppress, or defraud another is inimical to that other's development.   There are to be no debts (Rom. xiii. 8) and no injustice (*v*. 10).   Within the Church there should be those capable of exercising justice.   1 Cor. vi. 1 ff.

(3)   Under the head of economics we may say that St Paul recognised that great poverty or destitution is an evil, and therefore inimical to the development of the fullest life; hence his anxiety for the collections for the poor; his exhortation to industry, 2 Thess. iii. 8 ff. Note also the exhortations in 2 Cor. viii. and ix.[1]

(4)   It is much more difficult to speak of St Paul's attitude towards the cultural system because the 'command of nature' which we have won, which we exercise, and which we are ever increasing, was relatively small in his day, and what there was of it was not generally so regarded or described.   St Paul never undervalued the advantage of knowledge, if rightly used.   He would teach man in every kind of wisdom; in Christ "lay hid all the treasures of wisdom and

[1] See *Der irdische Besitz im Neuen Testament*, by Christian Rogge, pp. 94–116 (which is extremely well done), *e.g.* on 2 Cor. ix. 12 ff. "Das ist ein ungeheurer Fortschritt auf dem Wege, für den der Herr einige Fingerzeige gegeben hatte, hier ist dem Apostel der iridische Besitz bereits wirklich ein von Gott gegebenes Mittel zur Erreichung Gott wohlgefälliger Absichten" (p. 111).   And again, "Sollen wir Paulus' gesamte Anschauung in Bezug auf den irdischen Besitz zusammenfassen, so können wir es nicht besser thun, als mit dem Wort, das seine ganze Ethik enthält: Alles ist euer, ihr aber seid Christi" (p. 114).

knowledge." He spoke frequently of the need of the individual exercising his higher powers to overcome the lower nature—the animal man; he constantly inculcates the absolute necessity of personal purity and social purity, of temperance in its widest sense, of moderation in food, and of this in social gatherings, and of restraint towards all kinds of lust or inordinate desire. We must, of course, remember that the educational systems of the empire for long after St Paul's day were in heathen hands[1].

Professor Giddings regards the development of the ' social man' as the *ultimate* end of an efficient social organisation. " If the man is becoming ever better as a human being, more rational, more sympathetic, and with an ever-broadening consciousness of kind...then the social organisation is sound and efficient[2]."

He then proceeds to state that he believes the following analysis of personality (which he does not claim to have originated) to be correct[3]. Firstly there is the merely physiological life; from which the facts of (secondly) the *mental* life are distinguished; within the realm of mental life, (thirdly) *moral* qualities and activities are distinguished from the totalities of ideas, emotions, and volitions; and (fourthly) within the realm of moral phenomena, the *social* ideas, feelings, and volitions must be regarded as a part of specially practical importance. Thus we rise from vitality to mentality, then to morality, and lastly to sociality. Thus *sociality* may be regarded as the highest develop-

---

[1] See Bigg, *The Church's task under the Roman Empire*, pp. 25 ff. (N.B. note on p. 25).

[2] p. 249.   [3] pp. 250 ff.

ment of the personality, and the social virtues as of
primary importance.

Or, viewing this sequence in the reverse order, we
see that the perfect social personality demands morality;
and morality, if it is of a lofty nature, demands reason-
ableness and thoughtfulness; and the power to think
and reason demands at least some degree of health or
vitality, the *mens sana in corpore sano*.

In Philipp. ii. 1 ff. the social virtues—tender
mercies, compassions, being of the same mind, having
the same love, being of one accord and one mind—are
dependent on the moral virtue of peacefulness ("doing
nothing through faction or through vain-glory"),
which is connected with a reasonable estimate of one's
own value which is the result of clear thinking—a
mental exercise.   We see a similar connection in
Eph. iv. (17–25); the Gentile life is the result of want
of thought and reason; this want leads to immorality
(and πλεονεξία is certainly an *unsocial* sin).   On the
other hand the Christian must have a different intellectual conception (*v.* 23); he must, in consequence
of clearer thought, act differently; the life of the 'new
man' must be marked by righteousness and holiness,
which are of the truth (and truth is both an intellectual
power and a moral virtue).   In consequence (διὸ) he
must fulfil the social obligation of truthfulness (*v.* 25)
in its fullest sense.   Again in Col. ii. 8 we have a
strong warning against false thinking, as also in ii. 22.
Then in iii. 5 St Paul passes quite naturally to a
rebuke of moral evils, and then to a warning against
certain flagrantly unsocial sins in iii. 8, *e.g.* ὀργή, θυμός,
κακία...; as a contrast we have (iii. 10) a renewal unto

knowledge, unto the perfect ideal (the divine image),
which must imply moral perfection; and, finally, in
iii. 12 ff. we have the social virtues and the social life.
Once more, in Gal. v. 7, we have a strong warning
against accepting the teaching of the false teachers,
their arguments, etc.; to refuse these will imply some
exercise of intellectual strength, as also of *moral*
discipline (*v.* 13); and to this moral discipline must be
added social conduct (διὰ τῆς ἀγαπῆς δουλεύετε ἀλλήλοις).

If now we consider the characteristic of 'Sociality[1],'
we shall find that, when viewed objectively, it is "a
cheerful and efficient participation in the normal
comradeship and co-operation of Society" (comp. St
Paul's frequent use of the term συνεργοί μου, also of
κοινωνός). Subjectively viewed, Sociality is "altruism
—thoughtfulness for others, sympathy with others,
kindliness and helpfulness toward others...." But
what is Christianity but the highest, purest, and
withal the wisest form of altruism? And are not
the expressions of altruism here indicated just those
factors of conduct upon which St Paul is most
insistent? Rom. xii. 10 τῇ φιλαδελφίᾳ εἰς ἀλλήλους
φιλόστοργοι, Col. iii. 12 σπλάγχνα οἰκτιρμοῦ, χρηστότητα...
μακροθυμίαν, κ.τ.λ.

The last subject upon which, in this connection, I
would touch is 'The Inter-action of Society and Personality.' As Prof. Giddings says[2], "The developed
personality, itself the highest product of social evolution, reacts upon society—influencing concerted

---

[1] Giddings, p. 259.   [2] *Ibid.* p. 266.

volition, moulding the social organisation, and in various ways modifying the social functioning. Society and the social personality are thus in continual interaction. Society creates personality, and personality, with conscious intent to perfect itself, shapes and perfects society."

This truth is capable of a double illustration from St Paul:—(1) The personal Christ is surely the perfectly developed personality; in a very true sense He was the product of an evolution, else what is the meaning of the successive stages of Old Testament history, or of such a saying as He came "in the fulness of time"? Again, what is the teaching of the Acts and of the Epistles if it is not to show the power of the influence of the personal Christ upon the Society of which He is the Head[1]?

(2) The object of the Society—as a whole and of each individual member—is the creation of perfect, fully-developed individuals who must in turn influence the Society. The work of the Society in Eph. iv. 12 is (at least mediately) πρὸς τὸν καταρτισμὸν τῶν ἁγίων, and the "unity of the faith" (v. 13) has at least some social force, else why the immediately following ἵνα μηκέτι ὦμεν νήπιοι?

With regard to the words, "Society creates personality, and personality, with conscious intent to perfect itself, shapes and perfects society," I would submit that one of the lessons which this age has been slowly but surely learning is that a merely individualistic Christianity, one which seeks simply to save its own soul, or

---

[1] The assumption in ἤρξατο in Acts i. 1.

the souls of other individuals, as such, is foreign to the
whole teaching of the New Testament, including that
of St Paul. No one can read Eph. iv. 13 and 14 (giving
to τοῦ χριστοῦ the meaning of the 'social' Christ, which
'fulfils the personal Christ' and remembering that
children are undeveloped men) without seeing that
the truth upon which Prof. Giddings here insists is
asserted in these verses—that society creates personality.

Let us again notice the double process mentioned
above, viz. that the personality in the society, while
shaping and perfecting society, is also consciously
intent upon perfecting itself. Is not this the meaning
of Philipp. iii., where the personal confession of the
earlier verses, describing St Paul's entrance into the
society, and his effort after his own perfection (9–14),
passes into the social exhortation in the latter part
of the chapter, expressing his efforts to perfect the
society ? This same truth is felt and seen with special
strength and clearness in the experience of the earnest
Christian worker: compare the exhortations to self-
culture addressed to Timothy (i., iv. 13, 24, 16) and to
Titus (ii. 7, 8).

Speaking of 'Association and Personality,' Prof.
Giddings writes[1] :—" Immediately antecedent to personal development are the cultural products and
activities. Back of these are the other public utilities,
and yet further back is the social organization. Co-
efficient with the public utilities, and especially with
culture in its immediate bearing upon personal evolution, is association, that continuing comradeship and

[1] p. 266.

interchange of sympathies and ideas...which is an almost universal factor in social phenomena."

Taking the first of these sentences we shall see it contains identically the same conviction which inspired Eph. iv. To see this let us work backwards from *v.* 13 ("the perfect man") to the immediately antecedent 'cultural product,' *i.e.* the "unity of the faith and of the knowledge," etc. Then in *v.* 11 we have the public utilities described in the organisation of the society—the different orders of teachers and workers: behind all these is the Church whose work they do and whose purpose they are effecting.

The second sentence, that dealing with 'continuing comradeship and interchange of sympathies and ideas,' need not detain us, for St Paul's whole life as a Christian teacher and missionary is one continuous assertion of his conviction of the need and of the influence of these.

The whole of this final chapter of Prof. Giddings' book is extremely interesting, and parallels between its assertions—the result of experience, inductively obtained—and St Paul's teaching may be found for every page, but I must not pursue this subject further. For I think I have sufficiently achieved my object, which was to show how entirely in agreement is the social teaching of St Paul with that of the latest exposition of the conclusions of Sociology drawn from experience, that is when studied by the inductive method.

CHAPTER VIII.

AN EXAMINATION OF SELECTED PASSAGES.

THE only way in which we can hope to obtain any adequate grasp of St Paul's Social Teaching is by making a careful study of those passages in his letters into which this teaching more particularly enters; I would therefore now proceed to consider some of these passages from this point of view.

St Paul's 'Social' Teaching is a part of what is sometimes termed his 'practical' teaching; we therefore naturally look for it in the hortatory portions of his letters. It is, of course, hardly necessary to point out that St Paul's exhortations are invariably founded on doctrine or principles[1], that his teaching upon conduct, whether individual or social, is founded upon his *doctrine* (or ideas) of man or of society. Each of the great hortatory passages found in Rom. xii., Gal. v., Eph. iv., Col. iii., 1 Thess. iv. begins with the word οὖν.

Where a passage, as most of these passages, consists of a number of exhortations covering a wide range of

---

[1] N.B. Bp Westcott's saying, "Doctrine is the fruit of history— enlarged experience—and is also the motive and guide of life, *i.e.* of conduct."

conduct, it is often difficult to discover one or two prevailing, or unifying thoughts or ideas, or one or two duties which are singled out as of special importance. But a study of these five passages will show, I believe, that thoughts about (1) the duty of maintaining peace and unity, and (2) of doing service, receive particular attention. And these two thoughts are frequently combined; not merely are they found in close juxta-position, but they are regarded as interdependent. Peace is a necessary condition for service being rightly and fully discharged; and self-sacrificing service makes for peace and unity. It will also be found that for both peace and unity, as well as for service, there is generally assumed to be a common underlying condition or temper, viz. personal humility[1].

In this connection we cannot fail to notice our Lord's insistence upon the need of service, unity, and humility for those who were to form the nucleus of the future Christian Society. And we must remember that when our Lord terms Himself the 'Son of Man,' He seems to identify Himself with the possibilities of man generally, and His conduct with that which should be the ideal for man. Two things may well be remembered in this connection:

(1) That in the Servant Passages of the second Isaiah the thoughts of service, unity, and humility are, explicitly, and still more implicitly, of frequent occurrence.

(2) The existence and cultivation of service, unity

[1] Upon the connection of St Paul's moral teaching with that of our Lord, see a detached note in Sanday and Headlam, *Romans*, p. 381 ff.

(or peace), and humility must, from experience, be regarded as essential to any highly realised condition of social welfare, or social well being. And so these three great virtues of the personal Christ—the 'One who Serveth,' 'the Prince of Peace,' and 'the Sufferer for the World'—must be reproduced in the lives of those who together form the *social* Christ.

I turn first to Rom. xii. Here the thought of *service*, nobly conceived as the practical expression of worship (λατρεία), comes first. This service, rendered by man, is the natural response to the love of God, expressed in God's service of man (ἐξ αὐτοῦ καὶ δι' αὐτοῦ, xi. 36). And it is implicity shown that a conditional result of this service, whether the giving or the due recognition of it, shall be *peace*, which is dependent upon conformity to the will of God (*v.* 2). We must not omit the strong exhortation to a wise *humility* in *v.* 3.

In Gal. v. ff. the exhortation begins with the call to maintain liberty, but the liberty of which St Paul speaks is essential for *service* (v. 13) and *peace* (v. 15), as these should be enjoyed,—as service should be rendered, and as peace should be felt. Here again the essential condition is *humility* (v. 26). The paradox—the thought that liberty and humility need not be opposed—possibly strange in a world containing so large an element of slavery, must be noticed.

In Eph. iv. 1 ff. the first thought is that of the necessity of living up to a 'calling,' but a moment's reflection upon the nature of this calling, as it has been defined in chaps. i.—iii., will remind us that the calling was due to a dispensation of *peace*, first between

God and man, secondly between Jew and Gentile.
Then in *v.* 2 the first condition of this worthy conduct
to be noticed is *humility* (ταπεινοφροσύνη, πραότης,
μακροθυμία) in all its forms. For the building up and
maintenance of the social body (the *ecclesia*) a richness
and variety of *service* (εἰς ἔργον διακονίας, *v.* 12) is
essential[1].

In Col. iii. 1 ff. the idea of the necessity for peace
and service is just as present, but it does not lie on the
surface. The mind must be raised to lofty thoughts in
a lofty sphere (*v.* 2); the old self, in which unsocial
sins ran riot (self-seeking in opposition to service, and
uncontrolled passions—the cause of strife), is dead.
All that calls down the 'wrath'—the opposite to the
'peace'—of God must be slain; anger, wrath, malice,
etc., which produce want of peace among men, must
(*v.* 8) be put away; national and religious distinctions
(*v.* 11), which also prevent unity, are abolished. In
v. 12 humility, again expressed in various ways, is
strongly enjoined and mutual service between different
classes (iii. 18—iv. 1) in the community must be the
rule of life.

The passage in 1 Thess. iv. 1 ff. is somewhat different
from the foregoing as it is interrupted by statements

---

[1] In a Note on the 'Ethics of Catholicism' (*Ephesians*, p. 271 ff.)
Bp Gore writes: "(1) Forbearance between divergent classes and
races and individuals—(2) doctrinal toleration—(3) missionary enthusiasm—(4) universal sympathy—(5) recognition of a universal
priesthood of Christianity—these constitute the moral content of
Pauline Catholicism." [I would note that 1 and 2 fall under the
head of *peace*, 3, 4, and 5, under that of *service*. And for perfect
service humility, as well as peace, is essential.]

concerning the Resurrection and the Parousia. The exhortation begins with a demand for personal purity; impurity is the wronging of a brother and hence an unsocial sin and therefore the opposite of service; it also prevents family, and so social, peace. St Paul next (*v.* 9) commends the high degree to which mutual service was rendered in the Thessalonian Church. Next we have an exhortation to industry for the better service of the community.   After the paragraphs upon the Resurrection and the Parousia, we have (v. 12 ff.) a high eulogy of those who do serve the community, followed (*v.* 13 f.) by a short, but clear call for mutual peace.

It is unnecessary to urge that peacefulness and service are essentially *social* virtues, they are practically inconceivable apart from the idea of a society. The service of God through personal private prayer, or the divine peace cultivated in the soul of the recluse, may be regarded as only so far taught in the New Testament as they prepare for a better service of the community.

Humility is also apt to be regarded as essentially a personal virtue.   It is really the foundation of all social service.   It would not be difficult to show that a want of this virtue was a chief factor in the downfall of the great empires of the ancient world.

Reviewing the conditions of modern life we can see that social peace is fostered and maintained by the idea or conviction of social service.   If employées felt that while they were giving their best service to their master—assuming of course that this was so—he was, in return, serving them to the best of his ability, we

should hear little of industrial disputes. Again it is
not difficult to see how large a place the want of
humility occupies in our social difficulties. Pride
causes all classes, except the very richest, to live above
their income, with which comes the temptation to
oppress those beneath them in order to accomplish
this. Often pride, the source of self-sufficiency, prevents men and women from qualifying themselves, by
study and practice, to be of greater usefulness to the
community. Again, when the seeds of a social dispute
have been sown, or the conditions of such are in the
air, pride frequently prevents one or both parties from
making those concessions which might terminate the
quarrel.

But a deeper study of St Paul's teaching will show
that both unity (or peace) and service spring from *love*,
and are manifestations of righteousness. Love is the
inspiring motive of both unity and service, and both
are prevented by sin, which is the great *separating*
power, and which finds its expression in different forms
or manifestations of selfishness.

[*Note*. In connection with this combination of
peace, service, and humility the salutations of the
Epistles to the Romans and the Philippians may be
remembered. In the first we have "Paul a servant...
grace to you and peace." In the second "Paul and
Timothy, servants...grace to you and peace." In
each case the grace which proceeds from our Lord
Jesus Christ was manifested, at least in part, "in His
humility."]

I would now proceed to a somewhat more detailed
study of some of these passages.

ROMANS XII.

The exhortation is based upon the whole previous argument which has revealed the Divine Self-sacrifice —that of God in Christ. Self-sacrifice on the part of the Christian (as a *socius*) must be the response to this.

[In xi. 34 νοῦν Κυρίου (which comes from Is. xl. 13) may well include this thought of self-sacrifice. Can *we* fathom its depth? Then in *v.* 35 we have a quotation (with an alteration of the person) from the Heb. of Job xli. 11, מִי הִקְדִּימַנִי וַאֲשַׁלֵּם (who hath first given to me that I should repay him)[1], which read in the light of this thought of the Divine Self-Sacrifice is very striking.]

If the interpretation of ὁ χριστός [remember δι' αὐτοῦ in xi. 36] as sometimes the [ideal] Messianic Society is correct, we have the thought of the Christian merging himself in the great Christ (Messianic) self-sacrifice, which may be regarded as perpetually taking place.

[Note that our bodies are μέλη Χριστοῦ, or τὰ μέλη τοῦ χριστοῦ, 1 Cor. vi. 15; again, in Plutarch λατρεία is used of a service of the state and therefore of a social service, and λογική is a sacrifice in which the reason plays a part and which therefore appeals to the mind (Mentality is a factor in Sociality[2]).]

In the words τῷ αἰῶνι τούτῳ[3] it is at least possible that we have a reference to Jewish teaching, *i.e.* the present age, and its condition of *society* as contrasted with the Messianic age and the perfect society. The change of

[1] (Heb. cap. xli. 3.)
[2] See p. 108.   [3] *v.* 2.

conduct, resulting upon a change of view, is brought
about by the action of the Holy Spirit upon the
reasoning faculty. It is through the enlightened
reason, which counsels obedience to the Divine Law,
that social improvement will be effected. This leads
to the next thought—the proving of the 'Will' of God
which has three qualities—ἀγαθὸν καὶ εὐάρεστον καὶ τέλειον.
Here we must note that the 'perfect' life, whether
individual or social, is that life which is lived in perfect
obedience to the perfect will of God. But the 'Will'
of God is revealed in the Divine Law which governs
the welfare of the individual and of the Society[1]. This
law is 'moral,' it is 'acceptable'—conduct ruled by it
is 'acceptable' to both God and man,—it is 'perfect,'—
it is the fulfilment of the idea of social conduct. The
Christian believes that Christ has revealed this law, or
at least has made its revelation possible; hence the
Messianic, or perfect society learns and obeys this
'will,' or law.

So far the exhortation has been addressed to a
group of individuals[2]. Now individual responsibility
is urged. [St Paul's writings are full of warnings
against the modern heresy that a healthy social
organism can be maintained otherwise than by the

[1] The moment the conception is grasped that the moral law, the
physical law, the law of health, the social law, etc. are all parts of
one law—the 'Divine Law'—and that the revelation of each of these,
in response to man's effort to discover and obey them, is a part of
the one Divine Revelation, then, and only then, the true place of
Sociology as not only a science, but as part of the one (sacred)
Science, is assured, and its infinite importance will be rightly
estimated.

[2] v. 3.

healthy exercise of every individual member.] First
we have a strong plea for sober thinking (φρονεῖν εἰς τὸ
σωφρονεῖν) in order that by wise self-examination, leading
to just self-estimation, each man may discover his special
capacity for the fulfilment of some function in the social
organism. The last clause of this verse[1] *regulates* the
fulfilment of the function, and is really a warning of
the need of humility[2].

In *vv.* 4 and 5 we pass again from the thought of
individual responsibility, to that of corporate unity;
and the unity is twofold, first towards Christ (the
Head), and secondly towards each other (the members).
The idea is doubtless partly that of unity in (or with)
diversity; but there is much more than this. There
is the idea of non-interference, and therefore that of
personal freedom [*v.* 4 (*b*)] to develop one's own
capacity, which ministers to the richness (through the
variety) of the social life. There is also the idea of
the essential necessity of each to every other, as well
as to the whole.

The whole picture should be compared with that in
1 Cor. xii. In neither passage is there any definite
reference to Christ as the Head of the Body, as there
is in the Epistles to the Ephesians and Colossians. In
both the leading thought is that of the *unity* of the
Christian body, and this unity is not realised simply
through the existence of diversity of function but
through each separate member fully discharging the

---

[1] *v.* 3 (b).

[2] If he be σώφρων and his mind is enlightened by the Holy Spirit,
he will judge rightly his capacity and power (Sanday and Headlam
in loc.).

function which, according to his position or ability, is his. The following difference of expression in the two passages may be noticed:—in 1 Cor. xii. 12 we have οὕτως καὶ ὁ χριστός, "so is the Christian (the Messianic) Society," whereas in Rom. xii. 5 we read οὕτως οἱ πολλοὶ ἓν σῶμά ἐσμεν ἐν Χριστῷ.

Returning to Rom. xii., we find that in vv. 6 ff. the life of the 'body' is described. Every one must mind their own business, but with an eye to the common need, and every one must do their work as well as it can be done. Also in these verses we have, besides descriptions of the method of use of different gifts, certain general hints and cautions which must be observed, if the true social life is to be maintained, e.g. "Let love be without dissimulation." So much so-called 'social' work is unfortunately undertaken from mixed, or with secondary, motives. A philanthropic purpose is all too easy to simulate. But the motive must be single and pure; so the purpose must be clear; it must be hatred of, and the desire to abolish, evil; consequently there must be close connection with all that is good. Then comes the idea of brotherhood; the very word is suggestive of family affection; and in the Church, as a society, the true family feeling must be nourished. Social workers to-day know that the weakening of the family tie and of family responsibility is one of the worst evils they have to combat; and that in the strengthening of these lies often their one hope of success.

I must not dwell at length upon the various injunctions from v. 10 to the end of the chapter. Every one of these has been proved to be both true and necessary, if the true social life is to be lived, and if genuine social work is to be done. The final aim, as we have seen, must be the abolition of evil. The work will require sympathy (v. 10), also humility and enthusiasm and the consciousness of its being a Divine Service (v. 11); it will require not only Divine but also human help, e.g. liberality and hospitality. In these days we know how readily people excuse themselves for not giving because of the difficulty of *wise* giving.

In vv. 14 and 15 we have another appeal for sympathy. In v. 16 for unity and humility, and this especially as seen in attention to details. In v. 17 there is a much needed caution that our life and our work shall be free from all suspicion of being ruled by anything but the highest motives and regulated by the 'fairest' (καλὰ) methods. In v. 18 St Paul again enjoins the peaceful spirit, adding a conviction, which, expressed in modern mode of speech, is that the broken law 'vindicates itself' against the offender, or that the offence against social law is ultimately as certain of retribution as the offence against physical law. The chapter closes with an exhortation prompted by a deep conviction:—if we believe in the omnipotence of the (divine) Social Law and the Divine Power, which works according to this Law, then we have no right to take a gloomy view of even the worst social conditions. Effort made in the light of the fullest available knowledge, and in strict obedience to the guidance offered by that knowledge must ultimately be of avail.

Romans XIII.

This chapter opens with an exhortation upon the right relationship of each *individual* Christian to the Civil Authority.

[When the Epistle to the Romans was written there was no question as to the right relationship of 'Church and State.' The Church as an *entity* had not as yet come into relationship with the State. Hence St Paul's teaching in these verses can only be applied to the right relations between *individual* Christians and the Civil Power. Questions concerning the right relationship of a Christian Community to the Civil Power—whether nominally Christian or heathen—arose later, but these questions can hardly concern the student of St Paul's teaching.]

The practical lesson of this passage seems to be as follows:—For the full development either of the individual, or of the 'purposive society' (and such was the Christian Community in St Paul's days) a strong external framework of social order is absolutely necessary: and, at least in theory, if not everywhere and always in practice, the Empire in St Paul's day seems to have provided such a framework. There must be security to person and property; there must be the possibility of an appeal for the enforcement of justice being practically answered; for neither the individual nor the society which has to expend energy on the protection of its life or property can be free for the useful development of the higher life. This is why during the process of war a large part of the life of a nation seems always to be arrested in its higher development.

[The social worker may as a citizen agitate and strive for the improvement of the civil law, but he must not break the existing law. In England social reform has almost always proceeded through the creation of a more enlightened public opinion. On the Continent, in more than one instance, social reform has aroused opposition and been hindered through raising suspicion of a desire to employ anarchic means and methods.]

St Paul's entrance upon the subject probably arose from his high estimate of the value of *social peace*, and from his knowledge of the evils caused by, and suffered by, his own countrymen both in the present and the past, from their want of a wise submission to circumstances which even the Prophets of the Old Testament—and they were true patriots—had regarded as of Divine ordering, and therefore calling for recognition in the conduct of life.

With verse 8 St Paul returns to his wider theme— the true (or ideal) mutual relationship between man and man. Here for the first time[1] in this Epistle we have a strong insistence upon that virtue which is the special characteristic of the social life of the Christian[2].

---

[1] ἀγαπητοί in xii. 19 is a title. [A title is often an indirect exhortation to the realisation of an ideal.]

[2] Amplifying a sentence in Sanday and Headlam (*Romans*, p. 376) we may say, "A new *social* conception, and a new standard of *social* morality, a new grasp of the meaning of the ideal social order required a new name, for a new name was demanded for what was practically a new idea."

There is a universal obligation to love, because he that loveth another hath fulfilled (the purpose of) the law. Translated into the language of modern thought, the teaching of these verses runs:—God has ordained for man's welfare a great, universal social law—a part of the one Divine law which governs the universe. The 'Ten Words' were at least a partial revelation of that law. The Sermon on the Mount was a much fuller revelation. The life of Christ was a perfect expression (or revelation) of a life—lived socially, *i.e.* among men—fully understanding, and perfectly obeying, that law. [To realise this ideal in all the varying circumstances of human experience must be the ideal of every member of the Christ-society.] We must remember Col. ii. 9, "In Him dwelleth all the fulness of the Godhead" σωματικῶς, as Lightfoot (*in loc.*) translates, "because in Christ has its fixed abode the totality of the Divine powers and attributes, bodilywise, corporeally." Christ practically recognised the debt and paid it to the uttermost. Christ is the end of the Law for righteousness. The purpose of the Law was righteousness, that purpose was fulfilled in Christ. "I came to fulfil the Law." The Law was fulfilled only through the infinite and incarnate Love. Thus love has been, and is, the only possible fulfilment of Law. The infinite righteousness is the expression of the infinite love. The breaches of law contemplated by the commandments quoted by St Paul are all issues of selfishness—the antithesis of love. They are social sins issuing in social crimes.

We may apply the whole of this teaching to the idea of the 'Social' Christ—the extension and fulfil-

ment of the personal Christ. The Christ-society must
fulfil the Divine Law. It can only do this by personal
and social righteousness under all circumstances. This
demands that no social debt shall remain unpaid,
for justice is the complete satisfaction, or practical
recognition of the fullest claims of others upon us[1].

ROMANS XIV.

I must not dwell at length upon the teaching of
chapter xiv., though it has an important bearing upon
the contents of St Paul's Social teaching. Its subject
may be regarded as "the proper attitude of a member
of the Christian Society towards matters in themselves
essentially indifferent." The importance of that attitude arises chiefly from the importance of maintaining
peace and *unity* within the Society. Then we must
remember that excessive scrupulosity and readiness to
take offence at least suggest the presence of pride—the
want of humility. As Sanday and Headlam observe
(p. 384), "the arguments throughout are, as we shall
see, perfectly general, and the principles applied are
those characteristic of the moral teaching of the

---

[1] It is an interesting thought in connection with the life of the
ideal society that love, righteousness, and wisdom approach each
other as each approaches perfection. [They are 'asymptotic' to
each other—they coincide when each is complete.] The more fully
this thought is recognised in practical social work, the better will
that work be done. Love must not be antagonistic to either wisdom
or justice. The ideal society, as the personal Christ, will be the
embodiment of all, because, like Him, it will be filled by the Divine
Spirit.

Epistle—the freedom of Christian faith, the comprehensiveness of Christian charity, and that duty of peace and unity, on which St Paul never wearies of insisting."

EPHESIANS.

On passing from the Epistle to the Romans to that to the Ephesians we are conscious of a development in St Paul's ideas and consequently in his teaching. This development is specially apparent with regard to his conception of the Christian Society. It is not necessary to enter here at length into the causes of this development of thought, though two contributory factors may be mentioned:—

(1) The Ephesian letter was written either during, or after a period in which St Paul had leisure for profound meditation, and so for contemplating not only the possibilities, but the inevitable further conclusions (or deductions) of certain truths which had taken possession of him.

(2) The Ephesian letter was written from Rome—the centre of the great Imperial system, and therefore from where the unity of that system would necessarily be the chief object in the view. The particular development in St Paul's teaching to which we must pay special attention is the expression of the development in his ideas of 'the Body.' In 1 Corinthians and Romans we have the image of the relationship of members in the body, and to the body. In 1 Cor. xii. 27 we read "ye are a body of Christ," this body being the *local* Corinthian Church, and this local conception

probably underlies the exhortation in Romans xii. 3–5.
But in Ephesians we have a new feature in the image—
the relationship of the members to the Head[1], where the
'headship' of Christ in relation to the body is asserted.
This thought we may say demands the conception
of the one universal *ecclesia*.   The relationship of a
Christian in Rome to another Christian in Rome might
conceivably be different to the relationship between a
Christian in Rome and a Christian in Ephesus, but the
relation of each of these to Christ must be the same.
In the fourth chapter of Ephesians the universal
Church is not set before us simply as an idea which
still awaits its realisation at some future time, but
rather as a body now in existence, as already realised.
Into this society it was St Paul's object to draw all
men irrespective of creed, or nationality, or education,
or social position.

EPHESIANS IV ff.

For several reasons a careful study of these chapters
is of primary importance for gaining a conception of
St Paul's Social Teaching.

With the fourth chapter the practical, or hortatory
portion of the Epistle is said to open.   Παρακαλῶ is
certainly the first word but οὖν is the second; and this
word again reminds us that we must not dissever the
practical from the doctrinal.   Hence we must not
separate the exhortations upon the social life from the
high conceptions of the Christian, or ideal society set
forth in the first three chapters.   But may there not

[1] i. 22.

be a special reference to the immediately preceding
words (according to the true reading), viz. αὐτῷ ἡ δόξα
ἐν τῇ ἐκκλησίᾳ καὶ ἐν Χριστῷ Ἰησοῦ κ.τ.λ. 'The Glory
of God in the Church *and* in Messiah Jesus,' *i.e.* 'in
the Body and in the Head.' As the personal Messiah,
Jesus, fulfilled the will, and so revealed the glory
of God by His life on earth, similarly must the
Messianic Society, the Social Christ, the Church (by
living according to the perfect social law) fulfil the
will, and so also reveal *in its social life* the glory, of
God. This thought probably suggested the ἐν κυρίῳ
of *v.* 1 (in the place of τοῦ χριστοῦ of iii. 1), *i.e.* the
society in whose life the Divine Lordship is practically
asserted. Thus *Gloria Dei vivens Ecclesia.*

For the realisation of the ideal society St Paul
again insists on the need of personal humility (expressing
itself in various virtues[1]), as a primary condition.
This humility will issue in self-sacrifice; and conduct
will be inspired by love, which is at once the motive
power and spirit of service and which is essential if
unity is to be realised. For the perfection of the
whole humility is essential, for it tends to remind us
of the whole; pride so exalts the personal that the
'vision of the whole' and the welfare of the whole is
forgotten. And the realisation of the social life
demands constant, self-forgetting personal service for
the community.

It will be noticed that here, as in Romans xii.,

---

[1] ταπεινοφροσύνη, πραΰτης, μακροθυμία. (The occurrence of this
last word in the LXX. of Is. lvii. 15 should be noticed. St Paul may
well have had this passage again in memory as he had quoted *v.* 19 in
Eph. ii. 17.)

St Paul lays the greatest stress on right "mental dispositions which promote the right relation of the parts to the whole and to each other in the whole[1]."

We must not forget to lay stress on ἀγάπη which is more than the atmosphere of the Christian life. Like fresh air it is essential to 'life' and is productive of energy [cf. Col. iii. 14].

In v. 3[2] the *Unity* is regarded as already existing. St Paul was a great realist[3]. The Unity, like the πολίτευμα of Phil. iii. 20 ἐν οὐρανοῖς (the realm of realities) ὑπάρχει. In the 'spiritual' world it is already a fact, in 'this' world the Church must ever be approximating towards the fact, v. 13. This thought is of importance: for as there is a divine law, in obedience to which social arrangements should ever be 'approximating,' so there 'is,' ideally, a divine model society to which the human society must ever be becoming more like. The realism is further heightened by the intimate uniting of the 'one body' with such realities as the one Head, and the one God and Father.

[For the 'practical' social teaching, the ἓν σῶμα καὶ ἓν πνεῦμα[4] must not be overlooked. As Dr Armitage Robinson points out, the modern idea of 'unity of spirit' as opposed to, or as a substitute for, corporate unity is wholly foreign to St Paul. No one more valued the externals of social, or corporate life than he did; viz. his estimation of the order and framework

---

[1] Armitage Robinson, p. 91.

[2] τηρεῖν τὴν ἑνότητα. Cf. 13 μέχρι καταντήσωμεν οἱ πάντες εἰς τὴν ἑνότητα.

[3] See Additional Note on St Paul's 'Realism,' p. 142 ff.

[4] v. 4.

of the Empire[1]. To use modern speech, the Church
is a sacrament whose visible unity is not only the sign,
but may be the channel of the one Spirit which
inhabits and vivifies it.]

In *vv.* 7 ff. St Paul passes to the thought of individual
responsibility within the corporate unity, and to the
source, and reason for the discharge of this individual
responsibility. Verse 7, I would render—'But to every
one of us (individually) is given grace according to
the measure of the Messianic bounty.' These words
must be closely connected with the Messianic interpretation given to Ps. lxviii., a quotation from which
immediately follows. This bounty (almost 'privilege')
is characteristic of the Messianic state, and, if not in
the same measure, is yet the portion of every individual
in the Messianic Society, and who is living under
Messianic conditions.

St Paul's teaching shows the falseness of an idea
widely prevalent, especially among the uneducated at
the present time—that a perfect, or at least a satisfactory 'whole' can be formed out of imperfect parts,
that is by means of clever or skilful legislation. This
theory is usually the weak point in modern socialistic
schemes[2]. St Paul expresses his conviction that by
no mere 'arrangement' can a perfect society be
formed of imperfect members, that is of members
who do not each discharge individually their personal
responsibility.

[In understanding τῆς δωρεᾶς of the Messianic

---

[1] Westcott, *Christian Aspects of Life*, p. 103.

[2] *Vide Historic Progress and Ideal Socialism*, by J. S. Nicholson,
p. 64.

endowment, the work of the *personal* Messiah must
not be forgotten. The δόματα in *v.* 9 are the gifts of
the personal Christ. The endowments of the society
are personal-moral endowments which can only come
from, or be received through, a personal-moral
influence.]

In *v.* 10 πληρώσῃ must not be overlooked. The
idea is a favourite one in this Epistle. In this connection we see the work of the personal Christ as the
'fulfiller,' *i.e.* of the Divine Will as well as of human
destiny. So to the Church, through His gifts, belongs
the fulfilment of His—the divine—purpose. Again,
we must connect the idea of the Ascension with fulfilment, in more ways than one, *e.g.* the local, limited,
material body was withdrawn that the non-local
immaterial (spiritual) body might fill the universe.

Verses 11–16 demand special consideration. As
the result of His exaltation, itself the result of
complete self-sacrifice, the personal Christ gives to
men various personal gifts, or endowments. They, like
Him, must also give themselves. He in them causes
them to give themselves. In the members the spirit
and the life of the Head are reproduced and so He can
be 'fulfilled.' We may say that the gifts of 'gifted'
men—special officers—makes service possible: only
through their service is made more fully possible the
service of each separate member. For the ministry
in the fullest sense is co-extensive with the Church.
It is also a ministry of saints to saints and includes
'every form of natural service.'

In *v.* 12 there must be no comma after καταρτισμόν.
"For the equipment of the saints in order to [enable

them to render] practical service." "Every member of
the Body, and not only those who are technically
called 'ministers' must be taught to serve." [Is not
success in equipping others for work and in getting
them to work, for St Paul, a test of ministerial
efficiency ?]

Here we must not fail to connect St Paul's teaching
(1) with our Lord's assertions in St Mark x. 45, and
St Luke xxii. 27; (2) with the whole teaching of the
Servant of the Lord in the Book of Isaiah.

The next clause of $v.$ 12 εἰς οἰκοδομὴν τοῦ σώματος τοῦ
χριστοῦ may be regarded as parallel with or explanatory
of εἰς ἔργον διακονίας. One of the works of the Servant,
Is. xlix. 6, is to build up [the spiritual] Israel. Here
the body of the Christ cannot be anything else than
the society which fulfils the Christ, and 'to edify' is
synonymous with 'to enable to fulfil.'

In $v.$ 13, in three co-ordinate clauses, we have
the final ideal,—the result to be wished for, and towards
which we must struggle. (1) 'Unity, regarded as a
goal to be attained'; 'it is a consciously realised oneness,
the result of faith in, and the [full] knowledge of, the
Son of God.' [Here is a great social truth indirectly
enunciated—that unity is produced by the same intellectual conviction issuing in trust or confidence in the
same 'Master.'] (2) The unity is pictured under the
symbol of 'a perfect man,'—'God's New Man grown
at length to full manhood'—the Social Christ; this
naturally leads to (3) The maturity (in every sense
of the word); and it is applied to the whole nature of
the now fulfilled Christ. The purpose of God revealed
in the personal Christ is accomplished; in the Christian

Society (the ideal Society) is the will of God for Society, and the divine destiny of Society, realised and fulfilled. [St Paul's 'realism' probably never rises higher than this.]

In v. 14, which describes the immaturity of St Paul's converts (νήπιοι), we have a striking contrast to the ideal of v. 13. The immature here are *individuals*, and through their immaturity are they incapable of being formed into—of taking their right place in—the ideal society. St Paul here again reveals the chief cause of the great weakness of modern 'socialism,' and of all those various forms of co-operation which for their success demand a highly developed moral and intellectual condition of each individual composing them. [The strength of a chain is only that of its weakest link.]

In v. 15 the cause of this individual weakness is still further revealed. The great enemy of social advance towards social perfection is private selfishness. [The verb ἀληθεύοντες 'need not be restricted to truthfulness in speech.'] The social ideal—the 'true' society —can only be realised when selfishness is entirely absent; for selfishness makes imperfect individuals, out of whom a true or perfect society cannot be constructed. To-day we see effort after effort towards the improvement of 'society' wrecked through individuals seeking personal advantage instead of (like the personal Christ) 'losing,' or sacrificing themselves for the sake of the public good.

Verses 15–17 also give the strongest possible denial to another common opinion to-day, which is an absolute fallacy, that a mere aggregate of individuals all more or less alike and all doing the same work in more or less the same way can form a society, a single organic whole, that is a 'body' in St Paul's sense of the term. It is in its solidarity and in the diversity of its separate parts (each part contributing to the society that which no other part can contribute, and each part realising the necessity of making this contribution) that a true society exists.

Then in *v.* 16 not only do the various functions of the various members come under notice, but also the *relations* between the members. And it is upon the ' supply,' or fulfilment of these relations that the welfare of the society also depends. This is a truth which is more apparent at the present time than it ever was before, and the need of its practical recognition is also greater, because of the increasing complexity of, at any rate, urban society, when greater and greater specialization is the rule[1]. The 'self-sufficing' stage of any group of the population has been left far behind. And the more advanced specialization becomes, the more dependent is every member of the whole for his welfare upon every other member, not merely discharging his particular function, but upon his maintaining right relationships with him. [The truth of this may be seen in the widespread distress caused by a strike not merely among those who are engaged in a particular trade, but even among those who are simply engaged in one particular process of that branch of a trade.] Again an individual, as an

---

[1] The differentiation of function is a sure sign of the development of such an organism as society.

individual, may live an apparently blameless life, but
if he does not discharge the various *relations* which his
position should entail, the result to society is disastrous.
Success in warfare will not be assured by the bravery
of each commander or each soldier—by each unit
doing its best.   It will depend on the perfection of the
relations between the units which makes the perfection
of the whole.   [And the evolution (or development)
of the Christian Society is a warfare against opposing
forces.   It is at least partially, as shown by Prof.
Huxley[1], a warfare against another development—the
'cosmic' process.]

In *vv.* 17–24 St Paul explains some of the causes
of the failure of heathen society, that is of its failure
to come to maturity, or to reach any satisfactory ideal.
The first of these is a want of 'thought,' a want
of serious intellectual grappling with the problems of
life, and of social life[2].   In the study of Society, as in
the study of Man or of Physical Science, or of the
Bible, the truth only yields itself to serious intellectual
effort.   [And all intellectual effort of the highest kind
is also moral effort, for it demands the exercise of
moral qualities, *e.g.* truth, patience, purity and honesty

[1] In *Evolution and Ethics.*

[2] "In all considerations of social work and social problems there
is one thing which it is important to remember—that the mind is the
man.   If we are clear about this great fact with all its implications,
we have an unfailing test to apply to any scheme of social reforma-
tion, to any social experiment—Does it appeal to men's minds?......
to the higher powers of affection, thought and reasonable action?......
Does it act as a stimulant to the mind, or does it leave it altogether
out of consideration?"   (Mrs Bosanquet, *The Strength of the People,*
pp. 1 ff.)

of purpose, and perseverance.] From neglect of the
duty of thinking comes the loss of the power to think
—atrophy of the thinking faculty—issuing in ἀσέλγεια,
a particularly *unsocial* form of sin, being callousness
of the requirements of even social 'decency.'

In *v.* 20 we have yet another contrast. The
Christ (τὸν χριστόν) is placed over against the picture
of heathen society. I would interpret this verse thus:
These processes I have been describing were not those
through which you 'learnt' (or were trained) to take
your part in 'the Christ.' Against this interpretation
it may be objected that in *v.* 21 αὐτόν and ἐν αὐτῷ can
only have a *personal* significance. This I admit, but
μανθάνειν τὸν χριστόν depends on having heard (through
the Christian Teachers, His representatives) the *personal*
Christ, and on having been taught (and disciplined)
through communion with Him, because the truth—the
'ideal' in its widest sense—is in Jesus. Truth is
embodied (incarnate) in 'Jesus,' Who is the Christ.

In *vv.* 22 ff. we have a thought which has met us
before. The change from the 'old' (παλαιός) to the
'new' (καινός) is wrought (mediately) through the in-
telligence. The mark of the old is deceit; the mark of
the 'new' is truth, through the renewal of the 'spirit
of the mind.' Then ἐν δικαιοσύνῃ...τῆς ἀληθείας is conduct according to the (divine and universal) law, and
it is such conduct in its highest perfection, for ἀληθείας
stamps it as 'ideal,' *i.e.* in perfect conformity to the
divine law.

From *v.* 25 we have a series of warnings and
exhortations. The warnings are against certain *un-*

social sins, the exhortations are to the fulfilment of
certain social duties[1]. "Six sins," it is said, "are
struck at—lying, resentment, stealing, bad language,
bad temper, and lust[2]."

Falsehood (I would rather say 'falseness') in all its
forms is to be put away because even for its maintenance, for its 'coherence,' to say nothing of its growth
or development, society demands ἡ ἀλήθεια. One
member must be able to trust another. The Alpine
climber who cannot trust eye or foot or hand is in
danger. Then commercial prosperity and progress
depend on 'trust.' Continued anger is a 'separating'
sin, and the devil's work is to cause divisions.

In all labour (and the Greek was not fond of
manual labour) there is profit, not only for self, but
for the community. We must work that we may
fulfil *social* obligations. Here, again, is a truth which
needs constant insistence to-day. Verse 29, again,
contains a truth—a warning—whose importance has
grown as society has become more complex, and as the
means of rapid communication of news over the earth's
surface, and to great multitudes simultaneously, have
increased.

I must not pursue this examination in detail of
St Paul's Social Teaching any farther. I hope I have
shown that if his language is studied with care he will
be found to have bequeathed to us a wealth of instruc-

---

[1] " Zunächst folgen (4. 25–54) Einzelmahnungen, Warnung vor
Sünden wider den Nächsten (4. 25–31), Mahnung zum richtigen
Verhalten gegen den Nächsten 4. 35–5. 2 " (Von Soden, *Eph.* p. 83).

[2] Armitage Robinson *in loc.*

VIII] AN EXAMINATION OF SELECTED PASSAGES 141

tion in this field. I hope I have sufficiently indicated
what is the general nature of his social teaching, and
how useful it will be found for the solution of present
problems, needs, and difficulties. In the commonly
accepted interpretation of the term it may be regarded
as 'prophetic,' that is, it seems specially applicable to
a condition of society which is ever growing more
complex. Doubtless the society to which the Epistle
to the Ephesians was addressed—that of the Greek
cities of Asia Minor—was in a degree complex, but not
nearly so much so as our own. The equal usefulness
of the teaching to such very different social conditions
is no small evidence of its truth. The value of a
theory, it has been said, depends upon the number of
things it will explain. In this respect St Paul's social
teaching is like that of our Lord, and like that of the
Hebrew Prophets. All reveal to us what may be
termed the *absolute* laws of the social world. It is in
this that the value of the teaching of all these consists.
The laws they state are, in the sphere of sociology,
what *e.g.* the laws of motion are in the realm of physics.
The truth of these social laws has been proved by more
than eighteen hundred years of very varied social experience. Obedience to them has issued in social
welfare, disobedience has been followed by social
disaster. The study of these laws or principles, the
clear expression of them, and their application to
present needs and difficulties is one of the most important tasks incumbent upon the Christian Church.

ADDITIONAL NOTE. ST PAUL'S 'REALISM.'

More than once in the foregoing pages I have referred to this aspect of St Paul's teaching. Unless we bear it in mind, much of the meaning of that teaching will be lost to us. It is very apparent in the Epistle to the Ephesians, and especially in the first three chapters of the letter[1].

By St Paul's realism I mean his conviction that all which he is labouring to accomplish already (ideally) exists, e.g. there is in the counsels of God an ideal society to which the true Christian Society must conform. ἡμῶν γὰρ τὸ πολίτευμα ἐν οὐρανοῖς ὑπάρχει[2].

If we take the first chapter of Ephesians we shall find there that entities, or existences, or processes, or relations, are asserted to subsist *apart* from time and place, but which have to be realised *in* time and place, e.g. the ideas suggested by the terms, adoption, mystery, dispensation, inheritance, calling, 'the Christ.' These are generally regarded as things to be realised in the future. This is doubtless true, but St Paul also

---

[1] "Looking at the vast body of the State, St Paul saw in the magnificent form of outward unity the faint reflection of a Divine archetype. The citizenship of which he had experienced the virtue at Philippi and Jerusalem and Caesarea, was to him a symbol of heavenly privileges in a more august body. In this spirit he bids the Philippians live as citizens of God's Kingdom, worthily of the Gospel of Christ. Our country, he adds, the holy city to which we belong, and in which we find the rule and inspiration of social duty, is in heaven, no creation of to-day or yesterday" (Westcott, *Christian Aspects of Life*, p. 103).

[2] Philipp. iii. 20.

regards them as existing now in the counsel of God, where they ever have existed. In this St Paul's teaching reminds us of the Platonic myth concerning the men who were permitted to look upon the sea of absolute truth.

Or we may express St Paul's teaching thus:—He is engaged in building up, not *a* society, but *the* society, whose pattern or antitype exists already in the Divine Counsel. The gradual creation of this society on earth is part of (or involves) the revelation of ' the mystery.' To the Divine pattern or plan, already in existence, the Church, the Messianic Society, ' the social Christ,' must conform. Before the personal Christ came into the world the Divine model for human life existed in the Divine mind. Jesus realises that model under certain definite circumstances and conditions on earth.

In Eph. ii. 10 Christians are regarded as instruments created for a certain purpose. What that purpose is, and why the instruments are adapted to the work (or can be adapted) are both ordered already in the Divine mind. The Apostle sees, and the Christians of Ephesus may see, sufficient of the purpose or work to enable them to enter intelligently and heartily into the Divine will or purpose.

The Hebrew prophets saw what social virtues must be cultivated and exercised for the realisation of the Ideal—Messianic—Society. Our Lord, Who was the true founder of this Society, realised in His own person an expression of these virtues. St Paul sees that He is not only the Personal Messiah, but that the Society which He founded in order to express and realise His will and purpose, and which is but an extension of

Himself, is the true Messianic Society—the social 'Servant of the Lord' to whom the prophets pointed, the society which must fulfil the purpose for which Israel after the flesh was called, but which purpose that Israel failed to fulfil.

But the nature of this Society, and the virtues which it must exhibit, have been ever in the Divine mind, and so the Society has also ever there existed.

Now the modern doctrine of Society, if differently expressed, is practically the same as that of St Paul. The careful scientific study of Sociology has shown that for the welfare of society certain definite ethical laws must be obeyed. These 'laws' have been found by experience to be just those principles which have been uttered alike by the Hebrew prophets, by our Lord, and by St Paul. We may call them 'the laws of Nature (or of God) for the social world.' And as by the inductive process the 'Science of Society' becomes more exact, it will be found that these laws are as universally applicable as are such laws (in other spheres) as those of motion or those which govern the incidence and reflection of a beam of light. Here again we have at least a suggestion of a divine 'model' or plan for society, to which for its welfare society must seek to approximate. What is this but realism? (*Universalia ante rem.*)

In the assertion of the 'realism' of the teaching of the Prophets and of the New Testament lies, I believe, to-day the most powerful of all 'apologetic.' We take human nature as we find it, and also the perfect human nature of Christ—the 'revelation' of the *real* man. We take human society as we find it, with all its imperfections, and with its existing laws and arrangements. We take also the 'principles' or 'laws' of social welfare, as these are 'revealed' to us by Christ, or as they are expressed by St Paul, and we see that these principles or laws are admirably fitted to reform and perfect society. Did society generally conform to or obey these laws, then social difficulties would cease and social problems would be solved. This is surely the true proof of the divine origin and divine nature of these laws or principles, and so of the larger message of which they form a part.

The advantage of this apologetic is obvious; it lies in the fact that it appeals, first, to a body of teaching which we have in our hands—the Bible, and, secondly, to everyday present experience. It depends for its truth neither upon the historical evidence for the miraculous, nor upon the authenticity of documents. The value of the documents, their 'Divineness,' lies entirely in their usefulness, in the proof that where their teaching has been put into practice that teaching has been shown to be true. It meets human and social wants, and it is in exact accordance with the inductively obtained results into the investigations of those principles upon which human and social welfare depend.

ADDITIONAL NOTE. ST PAUL AND SLAVERY.

The subject of St Paul's conception of slavery,—his whole treatment of the question,—cannot be ignored in a work dealing with his Social Teaching. But the whole subject has been treated so frequently and so admirably elsewhere[1] that I have not considered it necessary to enter into it at any great length.

It has often been noticed that, while St Paul makes no direct attack upon the system, his teaching pursued to its logical conclusion renders it impossible for the system to exist, for it undermined the conceptions, and so the possibilities, upon which the system rested.

Slavery assumes the existence in a community of a class of men and women *essentially* different from the rest[2], and justifies an essentially different conception of their position and treatment. By these service was to be rendered, and from them it was to be compulsorily exacted. St Paul regarded the rendering of service as essential not only for the welfare of society, but for the welfare of the individual who rendered it. The man who does not render service defeats the possibility of his own highest development. But this service must be willing; it is of a moral nature, therefore a man must be free to render it or not. It must also be mutual.

---

[1] In Lightfoot's Introduction to the *Ep. to Philemon*; in Dale's *Ephesians*, pp. 398 ff.; Bp Gore's *Ephesians*, pp. 233 ff. Also G. B. Stevens' *Theology of the N.T.* p. 451 (from Dr Stevens' *conclusions* I desire to say I strongly dissent).

Upon slavery (in that age, generally, and in connection with the Church) see also Dill, *Roman Society from Nero to Marc. Aurel.* N.B. p. 12, "No modern has more clearly discerned the far-reaching curse of slavery" (than Seneca); the reference is to *De Ira*, iii. 35. See also Bigg, *The Church's Task*, pp. 111 ff. Note especially Arm. Robinson's *Ephesians*, pp. 128–129.

[2] Arist. *Ethics*, i. 5.

As Christ's service to us must call out our service to
Him[1], so must we mutually seek to serve one another[2].
This is essential for the well-being of society, Gal. v. 13 ff.
A Christian, because he is a Christian, is not only the
servant of Christ but of his fellow-men. [When you
make an institution *universal*, you thereby prevent
it from having in itself any relative social degrada-
tion.]

If we remember that the object of society is the
development (unto perfection) of the individual, we
shall see that no social constitution can be regarded
as satisfactory which contemplates slavery (as generally
understood) otherwise than as an institution to be
abolished. The slave cannot fulfil the conception of
the *socius*, for the very idea of the *socius* is of one
voluntarily and mutually receiving and conferring
benefits; also of one who has both infinite rights
and infinite responsibilities. The slave had no rights,
in consequence he disregarded his responsibilities. Now
the end of a social organisation cannot be that one part
of its members should be regarded as essentially different
from others, and that this difference should be regarded
as permanent.

Then again the Gospel has exalted *work*[3], and
ennobled the idea of work; and if service[4] is the

[1] Phil. ii. 5. [2] Gal. vi. 2.
[3] 1 Thess. iv. 11; 2 Thess. iii. 10–13; cf. 1 Thess. ii. 9; 2 Cor.
xii. 13 ff.
[4] St Mark x. 44 ἔσται πάντων δοῦλος.

claim to the highest honour and respect, then the 'workers' cannot be regarded as a class apart and to be despised. Doubtless the modified form of slavery current among the Jews as compared with that in *e.g.* the Roman world, and the higher conception of hand-labour among the Jews, were steps in the preparation for the conceptions which the Gospel has made prevalent.

EPILOGUE.

THE contents of the foregoing pages rest upon the assumption that there is a Christian 'Philosophy of Society,' though I do not here commit myself to any assertion as to whether that philosophy ever has been, or can even now be, *adequately* expressed.

At the present time we make use, if sometimes somewhat loosely, of such terms as 'the Science of Society,' 'Sociology[1],' 'the Philosophy of Society,' and even 'the Metaphysic[2] of Society.' The 'student' of society, in the widest sense of the term, cannot afford to ignore any of the conceptions which these terms are designed to express. He must know something of social Science and social Philosophy, as well as of social Economics, and of what may be termed social Politics[3].

[1] See p. 90.

[2] "It may seem strange...to speak of a metaphysic of social life. Society, we are apt to think, is simply an aggregation of individual human beings, and there are no metaphysical principles involved in its structure....We shall see reason to believe this is not the case; but that in a sense the structure of society must rather be regarded as logically prior to the existence of an individual human being. If this is the case, it is easy to see there may be a metaphysic of it" (Mackenzie, *Social Philosophy*, p. 31).

[3] See an essay by E. J. Urwick in Loch's *Methods of Social Advance*.

Of the 'Science' of Society, and of 'Sociology,' as these terms are understood to-day, we may say that the New Testament knows nothing. The ideas which we connect with them were foreign to that age; they imply an attitude of mind which was not that of the New Testament writers.

When the scientific sociologist to-day speaks of sociological 'Laws' he would claim, and, I believe, quite justifiably, that between such laws of this science as have been discovered, and wider laws that prevail throughout the universe[1], there are relations which can already be perceived, e.g. the law of the tendency to movement along the line of least resistance.

I know, of course, that there are still many who would deny to sociology a place beside such sciences as geology, palaeontology, biology and physiology. Some would deny such a place to psychology; and still more numerous are those who would deny a similar place to ethics.

But in the light of the experience of the recent past such denials seem at least rash. Doubtless the study of these subjects from the strictly scientific point of view is comparatively recent [by 'scientific' I mean 'objectively' and by the method of induction], and many of the conclusions which we term their 'laws' must still be regarded as only tentatively true. Before we can speak of these laws with the same degree of certainty with which we speak of the laws of some of the physical sciences, the mass of materials to hand, from which we may draw conclusions, will have to be

[1] See Giddings, *Elements of Sociology*, p. 330.

enormously increased, and these materials will have to be examined with much greater care[1].

As inductive sciences, sociology, psychology, and ethics, are yet in their childhood. But we must not judge of the position of these sciences in the world of thought and knowledge generally by their present position in England. In America, in France, and in Germany their estimation and recognition are very different from what these are in this country.

A recent French work (which has been translated into English) is that by Prof. Lévy-Bruhl of Paris, who writes, "We have no desire to add to the number of works in which the definition, the characteristics, the possibility, and the legitimacy of sociology has been so often examined. Essays of that kind have only one time and that time is over....A science proves its legitimacy by the simple fact of its existence and progress....The representatives of scientific Sociology have wisely determined to support their teaching by effective works rather than by abstract reasoning" (p. 20). In speaking of ethics Prof. Lévy-Bruhl writes, "Henceforward speculative effort will no longer consist in determining 'what ought to be,' that is in prescribing. It will, as in every science, bear on a given objective reality, that is on ethical facts, and on other social facts inseparable from them....Arrived at a certain degree of development, that knowledge will render it possible to act in a methodical and rational fashion on

---

[1] As an indication of what must be done, see the Tables appended to an English translation of the First Appendix of *Les Français d'aujourd'hui*, by M. Edmund Demolins.

the phenomena the laws of which it has discovered"
(pp. 26–27)[1].

In at least two spheres of social conduct—those of
education and charity—men are beginning to see that
they must proceed in obedience to certain laws, if
human and social welfare is to be ensured, so far as it is
possible to ensure it. Speaking of what he terms special
sociological sciences (such as education and charity),
Prof. Lévy-Bruhl writes, "Later on, in a future of which
we are hardly permitted to obtain a glimpse, those
sciences will be sufficiently advanced to render applications possible. Rational arts will appear, giving
men a power over 'social' nature, analogous, if not
equal, to that which he already exercises over physical
'nature.' We already see some feeble beginnings in
pedagogy and in social economy" (p. 230).

If, then, we consider the position at the present
time we find ourselves in an atmosphere of thought
where 'scientific' method is being pursued, and where
we have already proved, or where we seem to be far
on the way to prove, that all spheres of knowledge,
including those of sociology, psychology, and ethics,
are governed by 'law.'

Now when we try to estimate the thought of the
first century, how does our modern method of study,
and our modern way of thinking affect our view of the
teaching which we find in the New Testament, *e.g.* that

[1] Contrast the difference in tone between this position and that
of the late Prof. Sidgwick in his essays on 'Political Prophecy and
Sociology' (1894), and 'The Relation of Ethics to Sociology' (1899)
in the *Miscellaneous Essays and Addresses*.

of our Lord, and of St Paul, in such passages as
Rom. vii. 21, 23, and viii. 3? Does St Paul here
(especially in vii. 21) use the term 'law' with the
sense, or in any way analogous to the sense, which the
term now bears in physical, and to some extent in
social, or psychological, science? On the interpretation
of this verse authorities are much divided, *e.g.* Sanday
and Headlam would translate 'I find, then, this rule,'
or 'this constraining principle.' They own that, 'this
constantly recurring experience' would be too modern.
On the other hand Prof. Denny writes, "'the law' of
modern science belongs to an intellectual world which
was not then in being[1]."

But if we assert that St Paul knew nothing of the
Science of Society, we need not therefore deny that he
had any philosophy of society. In an additional note in
their *Romans*, Sanday and Headlam assert[2], "St Paul
sees a plan or purpose in history; in fact he has a
philosophy of history." I would venture to assert with
equal certainty that St Paul has a 'philosophy of
society.' They refer to the word 'mystery' (*e.g.* in
Eph. i. 4-11), a plan which God had before the "foundation of the world." I would assert that part of the
contents of this mystery were the conditions, both
individual and social, of the highest human welfare—
God's will and purpose not only for man, but for
society. This mystery is not very different from the
Divine Wisdom, declared, as far as the individual is
concerned, in the life and teaching of the personal
Christ, and meant to be declared as far as the social

---

[1] *Hastings' Bib. Dict.* iii. p. 78.   [2] pp. 342 ff.

is concerned, in the life and teaching of the Christ-society.

I would now assert that between the teaching either of modern social science or of modern social philosophy and the teaching of our Lord and of St Paul there are many and close coincidences; and I would approach the subject thus:—

(1) Our Lord and St Paul *reveal* the great fundamental and universal laws, or doctrines, or precepts of individual and social welfare. (2) Modern science seeks by investigation, inductively pursued, to *discover* these laws or principles. So far as investigation has been able to do this the *dicta* of our Lord and St Paul have been proved to be absolutely true.

Will any one to-day venture to doubt the truth of, or to refute, the following assertions?

[N.B. All these assertions are 'ethical.' Some are almost purely personal, others are almost as surely social; but in ethics the dividing line between the personal and the social cannot be firmly drawn. The ethical 'society' demands ethical qualities in those who compose it.]

Sayings of Our Lord.

These are generally couched in the form of assertions of truths.

(a) *Mainly personal.*

(1) " Blessed are the pure in heart[1]."
i.e. The need of a ' single,' direct purpose or aim in life and conduct.

[1] St Matt. v. 8.

(2) "The disciple is not above his master[1]," etc.
i.e. No man rises higher than the purpose or ideal
which he sets himself.

(3) "He that humbleth himself shall be exalted[2]."
i.e. Attention to what are termed 'insignificant' details,
patience and perseverance are essential to true success.

(4) "Where thy treasure is there will thy heart
be also[3]" (R.V.).
i.e. Upon what a man sets most value, upon that will
his attention, and so his efforts to obtain, or attain, it,
be fixed.

(β) *Capable of both a personal and social
application.*

(1) "Blessed are the meek[4]," etc.
i.e. Welfare, or success, largely depends upon not
unnecessarily provoking opposition; cf. 'manner is a
great matter.'

(2) "Blessed are the merciful[5]," etc.
i.e. Examples of kindness and philanthropy, which
show the value and attractiveness of these virtues,
create an 'atmosphere' of the same.

Cf. "With what measure ye mete," etc.
The habit of demanding the utmost, or of giving the
least, tends, from motives of self-defence, to call forth
the same habit or 'spirit,' and so to create an atmosphere
in which this spirit rules.

(3) "Where the carcase is, there will the vultures
be gathered together[6]."
i.e. An individual or a society from which life (in its

---

[1] St Matt. x. 24.   [2] St Luke xiv. 11.
[3] St Matt. vi. 21.   [4] St Matt. v. 5.
[5] St Matt. v. 7.   [6] St Matt. xxiv. 28.

highest sense) is departing or has departed is not only a source of corruption which may spread, but is a natural prey to the lower passions of other individuals or societies.

(4) "To whomsoever much is given, of him shall much be required; and to whom they commit much, of him will they ask the more[1]."

i.e. The possession of wealth (or ability), whether in money, position, knowledge, influence, experience, etc., must, for the welfare of the individual and community alike, be regarded as a stewardship, and the natural sense of justice demands proportionate liberality in its discharge.

(γ) *Mainly social.*

(1) "Blessed are the peacemakers[2]," etc.
i.e. The welfare and progress (υἱοί) of the community demands the general cultivation of the peaceful temper.

(2) "He that would be great among you let him be your servant[3]."
i.e. The qualification for position, or estimation, in the community must be that of service done, or being done, for the community.

(3) "Neither do men put new wine into old wineskins[4]," etc.
i.e. The advent and acceptance of new ideas demand new methods of organisation of society for their realisation and expression.

---

[1] St Matt. xii. 48.
[2] St Matt. v. 9.
[3] St Matt. xx. 26.
[4] St Matt. ix. 17.

(4) " Every kingdom divided against itself is
brought to desolation[1]," etc.

i.e. Unity of spirit and purpose as well as mutual
subordination is necessary for the welfare of every
community.

The above are only a small selection of the
'universal and absolute laws' for the individual and
for society which may be gathered from our Lord's
teaching.

St Paul's method of expression in his ethical-social
teaching is somewhat different to our Lord's. He
frequently puts forward positive enactments or com-
mands, rather than states some condition universally
necessary, for social welfare. The following are again
only a few examples which might be many times
multiplied. [I have as far as possible chosen instances
to which I have not previously referred.]

[Two other thoughts may be remembered in regard
to St Paul's sayings :—(1) Frequently they are in sub-
stance the same as our Lord's—they enunciate the
same truth or express the same principle. (2) Very
often they are somewhat less comprehensive than our
Lord's sayings.]

(1) " The entire law is summarily performed in
the observance of one precept[2]." Cf. St
Matt. vii. 12.

i.e. The whole obligation which exists between members of the community is discharged by treating others
as we would be treated. [Presuming of course that

---

[1] St Matt. xii. 25.   [2] Gal. v. 14.

we knew what was the absolutely best for ourselves
under the circumstances.]

    (2)   "Bear ye one another's burdens and so
            (rigorously) fulfil the law of (the) Christ
            (society)[1]."

The duty of mutual self-sacrifice issuing in mutual
help, and mutual service.

    (3)   "Know ye not that the unrighteous ($\mathring{a}\delta\iota\kappa o\iota$)
            shall not inherit the Kingdom of God?
            Be not deceived, neither fornicators, nor...
            shall inherit the Kingdom of God[2]."

(The Kingdom of God = the ideal social state.)   Social
welfare is impossible where these unsocial sins exist,
and inevitably issue in unsocial crimes.

    (4)   "If I have the gift of prophecy...it profiteth
            me nothing[3]."

i.e. The fulness of the powers of exhortation and knowledge, and the most liberal almsgiving are useless
unless they are exercised from the right motive and
done in the right spirit.

    (5)   "Admonish the disorderly[4]," etc.

i.e. By exercise of the opposite virtues such evils as
$\dot{a}\tau a\xi\acute{\iota}a$ κ.τ.λ. must be eradicated from the community.

    (6)   "If any will not work[5]," etc.

The unsocial sin of idleness must be eradicated from
the community by the sternest measures.

    An admirable description of the manner in which
the points of view of revelation and inductive investi-

---

[1] Gal. vi. 2.   [2] 1 Cor. vi. 9, 10.
[3] 1 Cor. xiii. 2–4.   [4] 1 Thess. v. 14.
[5] 2 Thess. iii. 10.

gation may be regarded side by side, and seen to be not antagonistic, may be found in the late Professor Seeley's *Natural Religion,* p. 21 ff. We must remember that it is more than fifteen years since the passage was written, and that the domain of what he terms Nature—that of the sphere of ascertained law—has been immensely widened since then. Had he been writing the passage to-day the increased knowledge in the fields of sociology, psychology, and ethics would have immensely strengthened his argument. I would draw special attention to the following sentences:— " Nature, according to all systems of Christian theology, is God's ordinance. Whether with science you stop short at Nature, or with Christianity you believe in a God who is the author of Nature ; in either case Nature is divine, for it is either God or the work of God. This whole domain is common to science and theology. When theology says, Let us give up the wisdom of men and listen to the voice of God, and when Science says, Let us give up human authority and hollow *a priori* knowledge, and let us listen to Nature, they are agreed to the whole extent of the narrower proposition, *i.e.* theology ought to admit all that science says, though science admits only a part of what theology says. Theology cannot say that the laws of Nature are not divine ; all it can say is, they are not the most important of the divine laws.... Making the largest allowance for discoveries about which science may be too confident, there remains a vast mass of natural knowledge which no one questions. This to the Christian is so much knowledge about God, and he ought to exult quite as much as the man of science in the rigorous method by which it has been separated from the human prejudice and hasty ingenuity and delusive rhetoric or poetry, which might have adulterated it. By this means we have been enabled to hear a voice which is unmistakeably God's."

THE END

For EU product safety concerns, contact us at Calle de José Abascal, 56–1°, 28003 Madrid, Spain or eugpsr@cambridge.org.

www.ingramcontent.com/pod-product-compliance
Ingram Content Group UK Ltd.
Pitfield, Milton Keynes, MK11 3LW, UK
UKHW020315140625
459647UK00018B/1881